D1319945

TWAYNE'S WORLD AUTHORS SERIES
A Survey of the World's Literature

COLOMBIA

Luis Dávila, Indiana University

EDITOR

Tomás Carrasquilla

TWAS 546

Tomás Carrasquilla

TOMÁS
CARRASQUILLA

By KURT L. LEVY

University of Toronto

TWAYNE PUBLISHERS

A DIVISION OF G. K. HALL & CO., BOSTON

Library of Congress Cataloging in Publication Data

Levy, Kurt L
Tomás Carrasquilla.

(Twayne's world authors series ; TWAS 546 : Colombia)
Bibliography: p. 140–45
Includes index.
1. Carrasquilla, Tomás, 1858–1940
—Criticism and interpretation.
PQ8179.C3Z77
863
79-9218
ISBN 0-8057-6389-9

To Enid, Leslie, Judy, Andy, Bruce, and John.

Contents

About the Author

Kurt Leopold Levy was born in Berlin, Germany, where he received his elementary and secondary schooling. He came to Canada in 1942 and obtained his B.A., M.A. and Ph.D. at the University of Toronto. Besides teaching at the University of Toronto, he has held teaching posts at the University of Arizona, the Universidad del Valle, Cali (Colombia), the Universidad Javeriana, Cali, and the Instituto Caro y Cuervo in Bogotá. From 1965 to 1970 he served as associate chairman of the Department of Hispanic Studies, and as chairman of the Latin American Studies Programme, University of Toronto. At present he is chairman of the Department of Spanish and Portuguese, University of Toronto. In 1964 a Canada Council senior fellowship took him to Latin America for sabbatical leave research on the contemporary Colombian novel and to establish academic contact with universities in Argentina, Brazil, Chile, Colombia, Ecuador, Peru, Uruguay and Venezuela; from 1971 to 1973 a Rockefeller Foundation grant enabled him to enjoy a two year visiting term in the Humanities Division, Universidad del Valle, Cali, teaching, researching and assisting in university development. From 1969 to 1971 he served as external examiner in Spanish for the University of the West Indies (Barbados, Jamaica, and Trinidad).

Levy wrote his doctoral dissertation on the Life and Work of Tomás Carrasquilla; his study, in Spanish translation (*Vida y obras de Tomás Carrasquilla*), appeared in Medellín in 1958. He has compiled a *Book List on Latin America for Canadians* (1969) and has coedited *El ensayo y la crítica literaria en Iberoamérica* (1970). In 1974 the Instituto Caro y Cuervo published his critical edition of Carrasquilla's novel *La Marquesa de Yolombó* (Biblioteca Colombiana, X). He has published widely in the field of Hispanic American prose fiction and has contributed articles to the *Encyclopedia Britannica*, the *Britannica Book of the Year*, and the *Diccionario de la literatura latinoamericana*.

He was the first president of the Ontario Chapter of the American Association of Teachers of Spanish and Portuguese (AATSP), vice-president and president of the International Institute of Latin American Literature, first chairman of the AATSP Planning and

Development Committee, first president of the Canadian Association of Latin American Studies and president of the Canadian Association of Hispanists. He served as general conference chairman for the sixty-first annual AATSP meeting in Toronto in August 1979 (the first such meeting ever to be held in Canada).

In 1967 he was chosen "Chapter Worker of the Year" by the Ontario Chapter of the American Association of Teachers of Spanish and Portuguese and in 1973 he received the Star of Antioquia (awarded by the Province of Antioquia, Colombia) and the Symbolic Hatchet (awarded by the City of Medellin), in recognition of his contributions to Colombian Culture.

In 1971 he was elected "Fellow of the Royal Society of Canada" (FRSC).

Preface

It is some three decades since my chance encounter with *Fruits of my Homeland (Frutos de mi tierra)* ushered in a piece of literary research which led me to do a doctoral dissertation on "The Life and Works of Tomás Carrasquilla, Pioneer of Spanish American Regionalism" (University of Toronto, 1954). The latter appeared in book form, sensitively rendered into Spanish by Carlos López Narváez under the title *Vida y obras de Tomás Carrasquilla,*[1] in commemoration of the centenary of the Colombian novelist's birth.

I gladly confess that when I wrote my thesis I was fascinated by Carrasquilla. On having reread him for the present assignment I am unrepentant: he still fascinates me.

However, in taking this second look (a reappraisal which was not at all agonizing but most enjoyable), I have endeavored to tone down the natural doctoral temptation to idealize, indeed idolize, my author. Carrasquilla himself was the last who would have enjoyed idolizing. That excessive flattery was alien to his temperament is born out by a letter in December 1917 where Carrasquilla comments scornfully on the "bootlicking" technique of certain politicians of which he thoroughly disapproved.[2]

In undertaking the present study, the first monograph in English, I am indeed returning to one of my "premières amours" and am doing so with undiminished enthusiasm. There is one central conclusion that emerges. The author's local color and regional speech are at best delightful "extras" which hold the greatest charm to those who are conversant with his milieu. However, Carrasquilla transcends the boundaries of regionalism because of his understanding of human nature and because he gets close enough to his characters to see them as individuals of flesh and blood.

It was that living essence in Carrasquilla's character creations, children and adults alike, that first attracted me to his literary world. It is the same living essence of the individual, the searching concern with his hopes and fears, his triumphs and his frustrations, which in my view endows Carrasquilla's pages with universality.

In my earlier study, I decided to group Carrasquilla's works according to theme and to discuss under separate headings those dealing with the child mind and those concerned with adult characters. I am now able to discern more clearly the maturing process that Carrasquilla experienced in the course of forty-six years of creative endeavor. I therefore propose to consider in the following pages Carrasquilla's prose fiction as an organic whole and to examine its evolution from 1890 through 1936.

It stands to reason that the creative curve from "Simon Magus" ("Simón el Mago") to *Long Ago (Hace tiempos)* did not lead uniformly upwards. There were, I submit, more ups than downs. I shall record the latter faithfully, although I cannot promise to be as severe as the author was himself.

The chronological approach shows three major divisions in the author's creative process, virtually equal in length, which spell out his maturing from master storyteller to regional spokesman. In applying this key to Carrasquilla's growth as an artist, I shall study novels, short novels, and short stories and leave aside, for treatment in a separate chapter, essays, chronicles, and sketches of customs, as well as *pièces de circonstance*—in short all those writings in which local, moral, or philosophical concerns supersede the creation of character.

In an era such as ours when literature tends to become increasingly *engagé*, because the novelist cannot afford the "luxury" of being a pure artist,[3] Carrasquilla's message is refreshingly aesthetic. His timeless pages record the human problems of humble people. Here is the principal reason, it seems to me, why Carrasquilla's prestige as a novelist has been growing steadily in recent years and will continue to do so.

Carrasquilla's works have not been translated. The main reason for this is doubtless the challenge, at once stimulating and frustrating, of his stylistic wealth, which at first confounds the non-Colombian reader.

Some four years before his death, Carrasquilla announced in a letter to a fellow novelist[4] that he would send him his short story, "In the Right Hand of the Father" ("En la diestra de Dios Padre"), so that he might translate it into the "patua yanque." To my knowledge, the recipient of the letter did not heed the request, and Harriet de Onís' perceptive rendering of "Simón el Mago" (incorporated as "Simon Magus" in the volume *The Golden Land*) remains the only "patua yanque" version of any of Carrasquilla's writings.

In approaching my own attempt to reproduce, or at least ap-

Preface

proximate, Carraquilla's literary flavor in "patua yanque," I feel as humble as did Peralta, the protagonist of Carrasquilla's finest short story.[5] I trust my critics will practice the other one of Peralta's outstanding attributes—namely, charity.

Sincere thanks are due to my many friends in all parts of Colombia for offering loyal cooperation whenever and wherever it was needed. I have benefited from their counsel verbally and from their studies on all facets of Colombian letters, as is shown in my bibliography. I am indebted to my sister and brother-in-law in Bogotá, Marianne and Enrique Wallenberg, who were never slow to respond to my clamorings for biographical or bibliographical material; to my good friend Pepe Mexía, a nephew and close associate of Carrasquilla's, for generously making unpublished details available to me; and to my graduate student, Jeanne Maillard, for helping to update the bibliography.

I gratefully acknowledge the support given to me by the Humanities and Social Sciences Committee of the Office of Research Administration, University of Toronto, and the Central Research Committee, Universidad del Valle, Cali, Colombia, for grants in aid that assisted substantially in the research for this manuscript and in its typing.

I am grateful to my wife Enid for patiently reading the manuscript, to our daughter Leslie for doing some of the checking and a major portion of the typing, and to my good friend Jorge Isaacs, descendant and namesake of one of the most beloved figures in South American prose fiction, who lives in Toronto with his charming wife María, for unraveling a few thorny textual problems. Thanks are also due to Miss Irene Kenyon and Mrs. Carmen Lipp for typing the final copy for the printer. A special word of appreciation goes to Dr. Luis Dávila, the editor of the series, for his many thoughtful suggestions, and to Mrs. Pilar Hedger, M.A., for her generous assistance in preparing the index.

I am happy to record that I have derived both inspiration and encouragement from the affectionate interest which my new critical sally into the world of Carrasquilla has evoked. I need hardly add that I alone am responsible for any errors which mar it.

Kurt L. Levy

University of Toronto

Chronology

1858 January 17: Birth of Tomás Carrasquilla, son of Rafael Carrasquilla Isaza and Ecilda Naranjo Moreno, in Santodomingo,
Colombia.
1874 Admission to the University of Antioquia.
1876 Beginning of Carrasquilla's law studies.
1876 Antioquia's short-lived revolt, led by the distinguished novelist Jorge Isaacs, against the central government. Closing
of universities causes Carrasquilla to discontinue his studies.
1877– Carrasquilla's tailoring hobby in Santodomingo.
1879
1890 Carrasquilla's *coup d'essai* "Simon Magus" ("Simón el Mago"),
written in fulfilment of admission requirements for "El Casino Literario" in Medellín.
1893 October 12: Opening of the Third Story Public Library in
Santodomingo.
1895– First stay in Bogotá and publication of *Fruits of my Homeland*
1896 *(Frutos de mi tierra).*
1897 "In the Right Hand of the Father" ("En la diestra de Dios
Padre"); *Dimitas Arias.*
1898 *Father Casafús (El Padre Casafús).*
1898– "Thousand Days" civil war.
1902
1901 "Money Talks" ("¡A la plata!").
1903 *Hail, Regina (Salve, Regina).*
1904 Failure of The People's Bank in Medellín.
1906– Employment in Sanandrés Mine.
1909
1906 *A Child's Heart (Entrañas de niño).*
1910 *Grandeur (Grandeza).*
1914– Second stay in Bogotá. Position in Ministry of Public Works.
1919
1915 "Autobiography" ("Autobiografía").
1917 Death of childhood companion Francisco de Paula Rendón.
1918 Marco Fidel Suárez elected president of the republic.

1919	January 27: Carrasquilla's return to Medellín.
1920	*Ligia Cruz.*
1925	*The Blue-eyed Boy (El zarco).*
1926	"Rogelio" and *The Marchioness of Yolombó (La Marquesa de Yolombó)*. Suffers first symptoms of circulatory irregularities.
1930	Beginning of eye difficulties.
1934	Eye operation.
1935	August 7: Awarded Boyacá Cross.
1935–1936	*Long Ago (Hace tiempos).*
1936	Wins Vergara y Vergara literary prize.
1940	December 19: Death of Tomás Carrasquilla in Medellín.
1952	Publication of *Obras Completas*. Madrid, EPESA.
1958	January 17: Centenary Celebrations. Publication of first-centenary edition of *Obras Completas*. Medellín, Bedout *(EPC)*.
1964	Reprinting of *EPC*.

CHAPTER 1

Carrasquilla and His Context

I   Antioquia

PERCHED on the rugged Andean mountainside in the northwestern corner of South America lies the department of Antioquia in the republic of Colombia. Its area is more than half the size of the state of North Carolina; its population in 1964, according to that year's census, approached the two and a half million mark.

The reason for its name has been vigorously debated: theories of its origin range from middleeastern through European to indigenous American derivations. According to the nineteenth century Colombian historian Joaquín Acosta (who seemed to share substantially the view of the sixteenth century Spanish historian Pedro Simón), the conqueror Jorge Robledo founded a city which he named Antioquia "after the famous Syrian city of Antioquía."[1] The renowned linguist Rufino José Cuervo suggested a provençal source,[2] while the geographer Manuel Uribe Angel traced the name back to an indigenous word meaning "golden land."[3]

"The Antioqueños, hard-working peasants and leaders with energy and vision, have excellent reason to think no small beer of themselves," observed Kathleen Romoli in her delightful book, *Colombia, Gateway to South America,*[4] pointing out that the department of Antioquia not only produces the best coffee in the country but also accounts for sixty percent of its total gold output.

Antioquia's success story began more than four centuries ago. In its human mosaic, it is generally held, Basque and Andalusian strains predominate, though there is the persistent suggestion—long the subject of lively controversy, verging at times on vigorous polemic—that a group of Jewish expatriates from Spain might have played a prominent role in settling the area. The proponents of this theory

17

usually cite the preponderance of Old Testament proper names among the population, as well as the significant use of such place names as Palestina, Betania, and Jericó. Certain physical traits, as well as a distinct business acumen and a deeply rooted sense of loyalty toward family and native region, are also adduced in support of the idea. Poetic luster came to the latter from the pen of the nineteenth century Antioqueño poet Gregorio Gutiérrez González and, above all, from that of the author of *María*, who in his magnificent poetic tribute to Antioquia and its indomitable people entitled "The Homeland of Córdoba" ("La tierra de Córdoba")[5] left little room for doubt about his own position in the controversy.[6]

Whatever the racial stock of the early settlers, they certainly were lured by dreams of finding gold. Gold there was indeed, but it was blocked by fiercely hostile nature and no less savagely hostile Indians under Chief Nutibara. The Spanish chronicler Cieza de León, one of the associates of Francisco Pizarro, conqueror of the Inca Empire, vividly recorded his impressions of the "very fierce and fearful mountains"[7] which received the conquerors. As for the indigenous population, the chronicler's blunt description held just as little comfort: "All the natives of this area eat human flesh."[8]

The battle was short and intense, and the invaders did not triumph easily. But temporary reverses were not allowed to hold up colonization. Soon settlements were springing up all over the area within an economic framework which was based on mining, hunting, and coffee.

It was a tough milieu, and the early Antioqueños were no gentle souls, as was shown by a popular ditty of the period which associated the bearers of characteristic Antioqueño surnames like Jaramillo and Londoño with "devils and demons"—"Jaramillos y Londoños/diablos y demonios." Remote from such coastal points of communication as the Caribbean port of Cartagena in the north and the Peruvian capital of Lima in the south, Antioquia was isolated from the rest of Colombia through the Andean mountain barrier. The omnipresent geographic challenge—"mountain above, mountain on the sides, mountain from the river to the sky," according to Carrasquilla's graphic description—not only strengthened regional unity, but also tended to accentuate the distinctive Antioqueño profile.

When independence came, early in the nineteenth century, the picture changed. Emerging from their isolation, Antioqueños shared vigorously in combat under the direction of José María de Córdoba and also took the lead in social reform.[9] With the growth of manufacturing, Antioquia moved ahead rapidly, and it was not long before the dreamy "Villa de la Candelaria" had turned into the bustling city of Medellín, seat of booming cotton mills and industrial hub of the Colombian nation.

Confining himself no longer to his native region, the dynamic Antioqueño came to use his incentive increasingly in all parts of the republic. Today people of Antioqueño stock can be found throughout Colombia and are easily identified by their distinctive names.[10] So thorough is this penetration that the late Colombian humanist Baldomero Sanín Cano (himself an Antioqueño from the town of Río Negro) remarked to me with a smile that in Bogotá there are "more Antioqueños than people."

For a long time, solid economic achievement, "more Northern than their latitude,"[11] seemed to stunt cultural endeavor. Though poets and prose writers made their voices heard and indeed some memorable verse and narrative lines originated in the rugged setting, such voices remained spasmodic. The literary profile of this remarkable region did not emerge until the present century.[12]

Antioquia, a colorful section of Colombia, "bottled up in the Andes and different in every respect from the rest of the country" ("embotellado en los Andes y harto diverso en un todo al resto del país"),[13] with its customs and traditions and its distinctive human stock, provided the exclusive setting for Carrasquilla's literary production. It alone formed the background for the uneventful story of his life.[14]

II *An Uneventful Life*

Carrasquilla's life was devoid of spectacular happenings. He was born on January 17, 1858, though, as he said later, "no mysterious sign in the sky or on earth had forecast the big event" (*EPC*, I, XXV). His native village of Santodomingo lies northeast of Medellín, but is almost 1,000 feet higher than the latter. Carrasquilla termed it "ugly, chilly, and hilly,"[15] a cross between an "eagle's nest" and an "arm chair."

Authentic details about his early childhood are scant. The first fifteen years particularly are lacking in documentation. For this period, the biographer must resort to the "Autobiography"

("Autobiografía"), which Carrasquilla wrote to placate a reporter's insatiable curiosity, and tap besides the countless autobiographical sources in his creative work. Carrasquilla openly acknowledged the "intoxicating delight" which speaking of himself afforded him. His works therefore may be expected to breathe autobiography.

His parents were Rafael Carrasquilla Isaza and Ecilda Naranjo Moreno.[16] He had one brother, Mauricio, and one sister, Isabel. The former died shortly after birth, and the latter, four years his junior, remained deeply attached to the novelist all through his life. Many of Carrasquilla's letters, revealing in their outspoken frankness, paid tribute to Isabel and testified to the closeness of their bond.

Since Rafael Carrasquilla's engineering profession tended to keep him away from home much of the time and the upbringing of the two children was left in the hands of their mother, it was quite natural that the latter should have left a powerful imprint during the formative period of the two children. It was doubtless Doña Ecilda who sowed in Tomás the seeds of literature which were to bear abundant fruit later on. The novel *A Child's Heart (Entrañas de niño)*, which is strongly autobiographical, reveals a striking difference between the boy's attitude toward his mother and grandmother on one side and his father on the other. His mother and grandmother inspire affectionate respect; the references to "poor dad," on the other hand, show more than a little condescension and seem to suggest a lack of communication between father and son.[17]

The house No. 370 on the corner of Bolivia and Girardot streets in the center of Santodomingo bears a plaque with the following inscription: "The Town Council of Medellín to the memory of Tomás Carrasquilla, Master of National Literature." This house, which belonged to the novelist's grandfather, Bautista Naranjo, was Tomás' home during much of his early life. His first important work, *Fruits of my Homeland (Frutos de mi tierra)*, was written here. It is safe to assume that Tomás received his early schooling in Santodomingo and that his first schoolmaster was that pathetic cripple whom he immortalized in one of his short novels, *Dimitas Arias*.

Besides Santodomingo, two neighboring towns were associated with this early phase in the novelist's life—namely, Concepción and Yolombó. Both figure in Carrasquilla's creative work, either with authentic geographic detail, as found in *The Marchioness of Yolombó (La Marquesa de Yolombó)* and *Long Ago (Hace tiempos)*, or

thinly disguised as a fictitious La Blanca, as occurs in *Hail, Regina*
(Salve, Regina) and in the story of "Superman" ("Superhombre").
Carrasquilla doubtless spent time in both as a child, though it is
not possible to determine exactly when and for how long. The
Criadero Mine, which appears as setting in *Long Ago*, is two miles
distant from Concepción and was worked by Carrasquilla's grandfather. When the latter decided to avail himself of his son-in-law's
engineering skills and invited Don Rafael to work in the mine, the
rest of the family no doubt accompanied him. Carrasquilla, in a
letter written in 1898, referred to "the Criadero Mines where I
lived as a child . . . about thirty years ago" *(EPC, II, 756)*. This is
the only documentary evidence I have been able to discover for the
boy's visits to the neighboring towns. Besides there is no more than
the internal evidence in novels and short stories, which testify to
Carrasquilla's keen interest in, and intimate knowledge of, the mining milieu.

The boy's early steps in "Minerva's Temple" appear to have been
less than successful. School subjects, he candidly confided, left him
cold. It may be argued that the teaching methods as outlined in
Dimitas Arias and "Superman" were hardly conducive to arousing
intellectual curiosity. His abiding love for books, "good and bad,
licit and illicit, sacred and profane" *(EPC, I, XXV)*, not only overcame the inauspicious academic atmosphere but seemed to have
benefited fully from a milieu where "for lack of something worse
to do, people read a great deal" *(EPC, I, XXV)*.

His closest childhood companion in Santodomingo was Francisco
de Paula Rendón, (another important name in Antioqueño prose
fiction), called affectionately Pacho, who, in the story "Simon Magus," accompanied Tomás in his ill-fated challenge of the law of
gravity.

III   *Studies at the University of Antioquia*

In 1872 or 1873, the family decided to send young Tomás to
Medellín to attend university. There is documentary evidence of
the boy's presence in the state capital, in the form of a letter to his
mother dated August 8, 1873. Carrasquilla's youthful epistle, the
earliest one which has been discovered, showed clearly that "Minerva's heretic" had not mended his ways. Dealing with his scholarly
activities at the university, or at least in a preuniversity year (his

name did not appear in the official registers until 1874), Tomás expressed fear that because of his persistent lack of application he might be expelled from the institution.

Evidently his apprehensions proved unfounded, for not only was he not expelled, the University of Antioquia granted him formal admission in 1874. His first report, dated Medellín, November 15, 1874, displayed the unimpressive academic record of a student whose mark in Spanish grammar was "fair" and who was decidedly "weak" in Spanish composition. The chief interest of this report lies in the following fascinating footnote appended, in his personal hand, by the president of the University, José María Gómez Angel: "The constant reading of novels has harmed this student greatly."[18] The president's lament provided a fitting preamble to a life in which "the reading of novels" and their writing appeared to drive out all other pursuits, except perhaps that of chatting informally with his friends.

In 1876 Carrasquilla entered the law course at the University of Antioquia, but again, if we are to believe a fellow student's account, he barely paid lip service to his studies, being more concerned with "his person and attire than his books."[19]

Antioquia's short-lived revolt against the central government (in which the author of *María* played a prominent part) closed down the university in 1876, bringing Carrasquilla's studies to a premature conclusion.[20] Physical violence held no romantic charm for the sensitive youth. Looking back sixty years later, Carrasquilla remarked with his customary candor: "I chose to hide out, since in these matters I prefer to have others do the fighting for me."[21] University lectures resumed after order was restored, but without Carrasquilla. He had had enough of the dusty tomes of Roman law and temporarily seemed to have switched to a new career—namely, tailoring.

IV A Tailoring Interlude

As far as I know there are two specific references to this unexpected turn in the novelist's professional life. The article "Diálogo de Piedra," written by an old friend, the late Horacio Franco, evoked Carrasquilla's purchase of cloth for his village workshop. Besides, Carrasquilla himself took pains to include tailoring among the various pursuits which he listed in an interview in 1936. The meticulous concern with his appearance which prompted Antonio

José Restrepo's above-mentioned caustic comment was in keeping with his general interest in people's clothes and his phenomenal memory in reconstructing sartorial details, particularly when articles of feminine attire were involved.

The exact duration of his tailoring activities is not known; nor is it possible to determine the precise date of his return to Santodomingo after discontinuing his law course. He arrived back in his home town in all probability between 1877 and 1879 and remained there until 1896. How long he practiced his tailoring skills in Santodomingo we can only conjecture. The well-known Antioqueño poet Ciro Mendía maintains that his father, who performed the function of circuit judge about 1880, had a suit made by Carrasquilla, but there is no further evidence to support Mendía's recollection.[22]

His mother's death in 1885—Don Rafael had died many years before—strengthened Carrasquilla's bonds with the rest of the family, above all with his paternal grandfather, whose urgings years later were to provide the chief incentive for writing a novel "about Yolombó and its Marchioness" (*EPC*, II, 812).

Though residing in Santodomingo, the purchase of tailoring supplies brought him to Medellín occasionally. One of the very few surviving "eye witnesses" in 1950, Justiniano Macía, assured me that when he arrived in Santodomingo in February 1889 to assume the office of circuit judge, Carrasquilla had abandoned tailoring and devoted his time largely to reading.[23]

Our author's timid literary beginnings coincided with a brief stint as municipal judge which apparently did not last a year. The prerequisites for that job must have been less than stringent, since Carrasquilla's law training could hardly be described as adequate.

V *Further Vicissitudes*

On October 12, 1893, exactly one year after the fourth centenary of the discovery of America, the cultural life of Santodomingo was enhanced through the founding of the "Third Story Public Library." It is difficult to account for this name, as applied to a two story building.[24] Carrasquilla, who had been instrumental in its founding, continued to give enthusiastic support to the new venture, as evidenced by the extant records. He even served for a while as second vice-president on the library board.

The minutes of a meeting, held on April 9, 1896, made mention of the "distinguished author of *Fruits of my Homeland* whose membership is a source of honor and satisfaction to the Third Story Public Library."[25] Carrasquilla's "Autobiography" cites the circumstances which prompted the composition of his first novel. According to the account, it grew out of a heated debate in the "Literary Casino" as to whether or not the department of Antioquia provided "subject matter for a novel." In other words, could the Antioqueño milieu claim to be propitious for literary production? The vast majority by far of the members took the negative view, and only the president of the group, Carlos E. Restrepo, and young Carrasquilla favored the affirmative. The sceptical members then challenged Restrepo and Carrasquilla to prove their contention, and Carrasquilla was chosen to supply this proof. "It seems," he writes in his "Autobiography," "that some were born to give orders" (*EPC*, I, XXVI). There was no doubt that Carlos E. Restrepo, future president of the republic,[26] belonged to this category. Carrasquilla honored his promise by writing *Fruits of my Homeland* "in the arcadian peace of my parish"—Santodomingo.

It was not his intention to offer the novel for publication, just as he had not planned to publish "Simon Magus." At his friends' persistent urging, however, he finally agreed to travel to Bogotá to see whether publication might be arranged. About the middle of October 1895—the "Third Story Public Library" archives and the records about book borrowings as well as family correspondence establish the date of his departure with some accuracy—he left for Bogotá. He traveled in part by way of the Magdalen River, a route which, in spite of "poetic islands and enchanted shores," he was soon to find tiresome. He reached the capital on October 22, 1895, and about a month later, in a letter to his family, was able to record with obvious delight that sections "of the great work" had already appeared. Early in December he announced the publication for the middle of January.

The letters to family and friends, which allow a piecing together of the circumstances of this first visit to the capital, broke off on January 21, 1896, though Carrasquilla did not appear to have left Bogotá until March or possibly early in April. On April 9, 1896, "Third Story" records showed his attendance at the meeting which paid glowing tribute to the "distinguished author of *Fruits of my Homeland.*"

Carrasquilla's grandfather, Juan Bautista Naranjo, passed away between August and September 1896, shortly after the author's return from Bogotá. His death removed one of the strongest family links, on which Carrasquilla had leaned increasingly since his mother's passing. It also meant a weakening of the ties to Santodomingo. Altogether, it seemed like the logical moment for moving the family home from Santodomingo to Medellín. Don Bautista's legacy provided the means for doing it, and the house on Calle Bolivia 45–73, which until recently continued in the hands of the family, was built jointly by Carrasquilla and a maiden aunt, Mercedes Naranjo. He, in fact, visited Medellín periodically to supervise the construction.

During 1897 his literary activities continued with two short stories, "Blanca" and "In the Right Hand of the Father," and a short novel, *Dimitas Arias*, as well as "Heresies" ("Herejías"), his first essay of literary criticism. "Blanca" did not satisfy Carrasquilla because of its spiritual orientation, *Dimitas Arias* he considered "less bad" and more in tune with his temperament, while singling out "In the Right Hand of the Father" as the only one of his works prior to 1898 of which he approved without reservation.

In 1898 he published "The Lonely Soul" ("El ánima sola") in the journal *El Montañés;* in 1899 "Little Saint Anthony" ("San Antoñito"),[27] *Father Casafus (El Padre Casafús),* and a chronicle entitled "The White Dance" ("El baile blanco").

As soon as the house on Bolivia Street was ready for occupancy early in the new century, Carrasquilla and his sister Isabel with her husband Claudino and her family moved permanently to Medellín. During this period bloody strife was again ravaging the land, the "Thousand Days" civil war, which had broken out in November 1898 and was not settled until November 1902. Carrasquilla was not actively involved; perhaps he still preferred to have others "do the fighting for him." Yet the war inspired one of his short stories, "Money Talks" ("¡A la plata!"), reflecting the depressing experiences of a recruit who returned from the war to a broken home.

A Medellín charity function in 1903 prompted the composition of the work which Carrasquilla himself singled out as the only one among all his writings which appeared good to him. The short novel *Hail, Regina,* which Horacio Franco termed "that precious jewel," seems to have been dictated to members of his family.[28]

In the same year, Carrasquilla made the acquaintance of the woman to whom he not only dedicated his novel *Grandeur (Gran-*

deza) but to whose friendship and personal charm the character of Magdalena Samudio in that novel is a distinct tribute. Susana Olózaga remained a loyal friend throughout the second half of Carrasquilla's life.[29]

The bankruptcy in 1904 of The People's Bank of Medellín, which played havoc with countless savings, jarred the novelist's "innate indolence" and compelled him, for the first time in his life, to look for gainful employment. (Tailoring really had been a pastime or a hobby rather than a serious breadwinning occupation prompted by necessity.)

In due time—Carrasquilla never was a man to rush things—he agreed to take charge of the supply store in the Mine of Sanandrés near the town of Sonsón. It is safe to assume that he did so reluctantly, given his habitual distaste for the discipline and organization which attended a regular job. His three years in Sanandrés (from 1906 to 1909) were essentially unhappy years. His desperate efforts to be alone, at least on occasions, proved in vain because of the many good friends who seemed to besiege him constantly and who, meaning to be attentive and thoughtful, frequently turned into a "damn nuisance." His solitude and feeling of isolation must have been spiritual rather than physical. He shunned the mine itself. A mere glance at the plan of those "dantesque galleries" upset his stomach, he confessed in a letter. To be surrounded by dry goods of all descriptions exasperated him, though he chose to make light of it. "I, Carrasquilla in person, am the bishop who officiates in this cathedral of food stuffs and of explosives" (*EPC*, II, 772) he observed. As usual, one must read between the lines in assessing these superficially entertaining allusions. Carrasquilla felt in a vacuum, temporarily doomed to an existence "worse than that of an armadillo" (*EPC*, II, 763). Books provided the only escape, as long as the "good friends" did not interfere.

It was true, however, that Sanandrés in all its exasperating monotony had one redeeming feature. By renewing his contact with the mining background and psychology which he had first experienced in Concepción and Yolombó during his early years, he enriched his sketch book of humble people and events, foreshadowing the colorful authenticity of such later works as *The Marchioness of Yolombó* and *Long Ago*. Besides providing environmental and human documentation, the Sanandrés years resulted in a set of entertaining letters which tell us a lot about their author. However, in terms of immediate creative endeavor, the years in the mine produced little. The novel *A Child's Heart (Entrañas de niño)* and the "Second Homily" ("Segunda Homilía"), an essay of literary criticism, both of which he completed shortly after arriving from Medellín, were the only pieces associated with the Sanandrés period.

The death of a friend, Amalia Salazar, in 1906 affected him almost as deeply as did that of his grandfather and that of his mother. Describing the personal loss, Carrasquilla confided to the Antioqueño poet Max Grillo: "In August I lost an incomparable sister— one linked to me by spiritual bonds rather than by those of blood" *(EPC, II, 771).* It was not often that the habitual scoffer dropped his caustic mask and laid bare his human sensitivity. His allusion to Amalia's passing away merits note for that reason.

In 1909, the Sanandrés interlude came to an end. Carrasquilla returned to Medellín and resumed the same pattern of existence which he had pursued prior to his years in the mine. The next score of years was bohemian in character; Carrasquilla remained in Medellín during most of this time (with the exception of a second, more extended, sojourn in Bogotá) and regularly frequented smoke-filled gatherings in local taverns where literary and social topics were debated against a seemingly unending "backdrop" of Antioqueño *aguardiente* (literally, "firewater"). This period and social setting were reflected in his second long novel, *Grandeur* (published in Medellín in 1910), which the exacting author dismissed as merely a series of "everyday and commonplace subjects, persons and happenings" *(EPC, I, 259).*

On September 15, 1914, the Medellín Daily *El Espectador* informed its readers that Carrasquilla had left for Bogotá the day before in answer to a governmental call to occupy "an official position." The latter turned out to be a minor post in the Ministry of Public Works which our author held for the next five years. The uniformity of the office routine was as little to his liking as had been the monotony of the mine and indeed not in accord with his temperament: he nostalgically lamented the fading memory of his sweet "Bohemian existence moistened with the Good Lord's *aguardiente*" *(EPC, II, 795).* The same as in Sanandrés, reading was his main distraction in Bogotá. For a while he even kept books at the office, but apparently could not get much reading done.

Bogotá did not impress him at all favorably. His second visit seemed to confirm the impressions gathered during the earlier trip. The milieu bored him; he missed his family and friends and easily tired of the people surrounding him. Such was the eloquent comment in a letter written in 1915, which expressed marked impatience with Bogotá's "social comedy" (*EPC*, II, 782).

In literary terms, the second sojourn in the capital produced a number of chronicles which appeared in *El Espectador* in the column "Native Chroniclers" ("Cronistas Propios")—first in Bogotá and about a week later in Medellín—as well as the odd short story. Perhaps the most significant literary product of these five years was a short story entitled "The Toy Gun" ("El rifle"), one of the only two of Carrasquilla's writings with a Bogotá setting.[30]

On June 12, 1915, *El Espectador* published the well-known "Autobiography," which was to become one of the most frequently cited sources for Carrasquilla's early activities. Birth, family background, Medellín's "Literary Casino," the genesis of "Simon Magus" and *Fruits of my Homeland*, likes and dislikes literary and personal—all these subjects and accompanying circumstances were reviewed by Carrasquilla with customary informality and candor.

In 1917 he suffered the loss of two beloved persons, his aunt Mercedes Naranjo and his close associate Francisco de Paula Rendón. Life in Bogotá was less than ever to his liking for a variety of reasons, and in one of his letters to the family, he raised the question of a possible transfer to Medellín. However, as a government employee, his movements were determined by the regime in office. With a presidential election imminent, there was no telling where he might end up or whether he might even lose his job, because of his proverbial lack of diplomacy ("I am constitutionally unable to perform that political operation called bootlicking," he confessed—*EPC*, II, 799).

The elections in 1918 witnessed a contest between two distinguished writers; the prose writer triumphed over the *modernista* poet, as Marco Fidel Suárez was elected rather than Guillermo Valencia. Carrasquilla, who once had mentioned the possibility that a victory of Suárez might even bring an improvement in his own position, abandoned the civil service shortly after the elections and returned to Medellín on January 27, 1919.

VI   *Final Years*

The house on Calle Bolivia (which since his aunt's death in 1917 belonged to him and Isabel jointly) welcomed him and so did a loving family. Carrasquilla was not to leave Medellín again. The final twenty years of his life were exclusively devoted to "communication." He communicated with the past through books, with the present through conversation (which according to eye witnesses could be a somewhat one-sided affair), and with the future through his writings. No full-time bread-winning occupation was allowed to interfere, though his literary contributions to *El Espectador* continued in the form of "chronicles" about Medellín or the odd piece of literary criticism. The short novel *Ligia Cruz* appeared in 1920; another short novel, *The Blue-eyed Boy (El zarco)* in 1925; and finally the delicate short story "Rogelio" in 1926.

The Marchioness of Yolombó (which he completed on January 19, 1926, according to the date on the final page of the manuscript), was not published in book form until 1928. Its genesis may be said to encompass almost three decades, beginning at the time when old Bautista Naranjo first urged Tomás to write something about "Yolombó and its Marchioness." The dedication is a well-deserved tribute to his nephew, Félix Mejía, who was untiring in pushing the novelist toward honoring his promise.

It was in all probability shortly after completing *The Marchioness of Yolombó* that physical infirmity struck Carrasquilla, putting an end to those colorful all-night bull sessions which for much of their success depended on his dynamic personality and his sharp tongue. While returning in the early morning hours from one of his regular outings, he collapsed in the doorway of his home. He was never to walk again.

The clinical history (preserved in the archives of the Saint Vincent Hospital in Medellín), recording the background of Carrasquilla's gangrene operation shortly before his death in 1940, suggests that "circulatory difficulties" began to affect his "lower extremities" about the year 1926. It may, however, have been a sympton of a sciatic condition which felled Carrasquilla, all but paralyzing him. At that moment his great popularity paid off, as his many friends and, of course, family members rallied around his sick bed endeavoring to continue the traditional informal gatherings at home and thus to ease his physical pains and his mental depression. The latter was no doubt the more serious factor. A sentence from one of the letters from Sanandrés some twenty years earlier might well have lingered in the novelist's mind: "What is this poor devil supposed to say, stuck in this hole in a worse fix than the armadillo" (*EPC*, II, 763)?

His literary production during these final years was small in number of titles, though it did include the monumental trilogy *Long Ago*, for which he collected regional detail with meticulous and affectionate care.

In October 1928, some nine months after his seventieth birthday, he painted this melancholy verbal self-portrait in a letter to a friend: "Here I am, a wretched cripple . . . in a mess . . . all I need to do is open a school and clutch a Christ Child to be like my hero Dimitas Arias" (*EPC*, II, 802).

Yet worse was to come, when this avid reader, whose eyes were his life line almost as much as his tongue, was deprived of his vision through cataracts. In accordance with contemporary evidence and documentation which I reviewed earlier,[31] Carrasquilla's eyesight deteriorated so rapidly after 1930 that, in composing the *Long Ago* trilogy, he had to resort almost entirely to dictation.

In June 1934, Carrasquilla underwent a delicate operation on his left eye; the right one apparently was irretrievably lost through a detached retina. The operation was successful, and Carrasquilla recovered partial vision in one eye, enabling him to read and write again. This he did with his habitual lack of moderation, oblivious to warnings on the part of relatives and friends who cautioned him not to overtax the recovered organ.

The years 1935 and 1936 brought evidence of official recognition in two ways: The Boyacá Cross and the Vergara y Vergara literary prize, the latter for the first two volumes of *Long Ago*. The Vergara y Vergara jury—Antonio Gómez Restrepo, Baldomero Sanín Cano, and Jorge Zalamea—was "unanimous and enthusiastic" in its decision to honor Carrasquilla. Unable to attend the ceremony in the Colón Theater, Bogotá, the novelist sent a relative and close friend, Miguel Moreno Jaramillo, to represent him. Carrasquilla's letter to Moreno Jaramillo, conveying his mandate, shed light upon the circumstances under which he "dictated those thousand pages while completely blind, doing so not in the privacy of retreat, nor to an expert secretary, but to anyone in the family at any hour possible, and in the midst of the din caused by children and visitors, by the outside door and beggars, by telephone and radio" (*EPC*, II, 806). The prize, according to Carrasquilla's graphic description, amounted to some five hundred wretched pesos, "enough at best, to go on a binge."[32]

Gloom was to cover the final years of his life. His physical suffering was so intense that even Carrasquilla found it difficult to make light of it. He did not write any more during those years, but read a great deal—preferably mystical literature, for which he always had had a distinct penchant—and chatted with his family and friends.

Hardening of the arteries caused gangrene to set in in December 1940, and the amputation of a foot became imperative. The Medellín surgeon, Dr. Alberto Saldarriaga, who performed the operation, informed me that Carrasquilla "came through surgery well but died a few days later from uremia."[33] The doctor also recalled his patient's "pleasant conversation" and his refusal up to the day before his death to take anything and anyone seriously. He added that Carrasquilla was the most "courageous patient" he had ever met in the course of his professional career.

Tomás Carrasquilla died in the Saint Vincent Hospital in Medellín on December 19, 1940. Hospital records gave "shock due to infection" as cause of his death;[34] the parish archives "arteriosclerosis."[35]

CHAPTER 2

A Human Credo

I A Plain Blunt Man

C ARRASQUILLA was "a savage in frankness and in other matters" (*EPC*, II, 769) in his own words, championing simplicity
and the golden mean in art and literature but given in his private
life to the extremest of habits. He once described his Christian
name as a verbal inflection,[1] indicative of his lifelong addiction to
the consumption of alcohol. Eye witnesses recall with amazement
his infinite capacity for chain smoking and for holding his liquor.

There is no suggestion in his correspondence, or in accounts by
others, that he ever seriously considered matrimony. There are
definite indications, however, that he admired women, and enjoyed
their company and that he was receptive to their physical appearance. Particularly details of dress captured his interest, and he had
a distinct gift for retaining and reproducing them. Both Susana
Olózaga and Sofía Ospina—two important and loyal friends in Carrasquilla's life—refer to this significant trait. He favored woman's
emancipation and defended unequivocally her right and capability
to challenge the male monopoly in the professional sphere.[2] The
same attitude prompted in his works the creation of a number of
feminine characters who are superior in moral stature to their male
counterparts.

Carrasquilla's admiration, voiced from a safe distance and reflected in his writings, did not change his deeply rooted dislike for
responsibility, domestic or otherwise. "I have neither wife nor children . . .," he observed in a letter to his friend Grillo, "and God
willing, I shall never have any" (*EPC*, II, 754). Once again, theory
seemed to have clashed with practice, testifying to his belief that
"in order to be able to think, one must be inconsistent and versatile"
(*EPC*, II, 674).

32

His personal charm turned him into a beloved friend, his blunt tongue into a feared adversary. As he suggested on more than one occasion, he might well have lost his civil service position in Bogotá, despite the triumph of Suárez, because of his chronic inability to flatter influential people.

II *The Open Letter to Dr. Castro*

Frankness was his motto in literary matters as well as in human affairs. An engrained sense of fair play compelled him to take sides in an incident which because of its religious implications had aroused public opinion, threatening to destroy a woman's livelihood and reputation. It involved Laura Montoya, the head mistress in a Medellín boarding school, and Eva Castro, one of her pupils. The latter, who was about to get married, changed her mind at the last moment and decided to take the nun's habit. At about the same time, Alfonso Castro, Eva's brother and a well-known Antioqueño sociologist and writer, published a short story entitled "Spiritual Daughter" ("Hija espiritual"). Castro's portrayal of a religious fanatic who abused her position to turn a sane and normal girl into a "pitiful and ridiculous fool" pushed fiction uncomfortably close to truth. Despite Dr. Castro's emphatic denial, the purpose of the story seemed obvious enough. It was so obvious, in fact, that Laura Montoya's institution was in danger of facing a general boycott. Confronted by economic ruin and personal stigma, the victim appealed to Carrasquilla for help. In handing, over Laura Montoya's signature, a stinging rebuke to Dr. Castro for insinuations which he considered unfounded, Carrasquilla was of course not only prompted by friendship for the victim, but doubtless also by another factor: Castro had dedicated "Spiritual Daughter" to the "lofty, confused and defamatory spirit of Tomás Carrasquilla."

Whether or not monetary concerns played a part in the writing of the "Open Letter to Dr. Castro," as the latter suggested in an interview in 1931, is difficult to determine today. Carrasquilla himself described Castro's charge as "falsehood" inferring in "Peace and Concord" ("Pax et Concordia"—*EPC*, II, 707–709) that he wrote the open letter "merely in defense of slandered innocence." Perhaps it does not matter whether material gain was involved or whether the incident simply provided a more or less welcome opportunity to continue his feud with Castro. The above-cited dedication shows clearly that relations between the two old friends were less than cordial at the time of the incident. Whatever the background of the immediate provocation, it added a brilliant piece of polemical prose writing to Carrasquilla's literary work.[3]

III   *Enchanting Indolence*

Novices in the profession came to Carrasquilla for counsel, and he endeavored to communicate to them his own love for literature. But again his urgings to others "to exploit that fertile youth and to write at least one book a year" (*EPC*, II, 810–11) did not result in a similar creative rhythm in his own career. The "enchanting indolence" which he was loath to give up for the sake of a few "wretched bills" required constant nudgings to yield to creative activity. His sister, it seems, was untiring in sending him back to his work. Another positive influence was his nephew Félix Mejía— a fact which Carrasquilla acknowledged in dedicating *The Marchioness of Yolombó* to Pepe, "since you have pushed me so hard to make me write it" (*EPC*, II, 1).

He was unconcerned with material success and totally oblivious to literary glory. Besides, applying his famous blunt candor to himself, he declared that with the exception of *Hail, Regina*, he could see little value in anything he had written. As far as his four major novels were concerned, he ascribed "scant artistic merit" to *Fruits of my Homeland* (*EPC*, I, XXVI) and was quick to dismiss *Grandeur* as a collection of "notes, characters, and details of our milieu" (*EPC*, I, 259), *The Marchioness of Yolombó* as "a conjecture concerning that period and its people" (*EPC*, II, 21), and *Long Ago* as "a humble outline of Antioquia in days gone by" (*EPC*, II, 807).

The bluntness and spontaneity, the quick wit and lack of consistency which lent a unique flavor to his conversation came alive in his correspondence. The latter can in fact be said to add vivid traits to the author's literary profile. Writing without restraint, Carrasquilla frequently confounded his correspondents by passing abruptly from lamentations to "foolish things." To conceal his human essence under a prickly exterior was an organic part of his psychological makeup—essential for an understanding of Carrasquilla's approach to life. He maintained that innocence in mischievous disguise played a significant role in the "eternal farce of life."

IV *A Plea for Tolerance*

Carrasquilla cannot be termed a social and political critic, although he did challenge extreme behavior patterns which jeopardized the workings of society. His chief weapon was devastating satire, accentuating his plea for sanity, genuine aristocracy, and a true scale of values. Whenever he came to grips with social problems, Carrasquilla showed himself a champion of democratic principles and a staunch defender of the concept that the aristocracy of birth and money must be replaced by that of merit. In the novel *Grandeur*, Magdalena Samudio, personifying that sound common sense which Carrasquilla admired, voiced his clear indictment of those who "squander millions in vagabondries . . . while allowing their fellowmen to starve . . ." (*EPC*, I, 352). When Barbara Caballero, the indefatigable Marchioness of Yolombó, allayed the worst sufferings of the needy, the author had this comment: "the destitute can hardly be grateful for aid. Whatever they are given they regard as restitution for the fearful way in which they have been cheated and robbed by the rich" (*EPC*, II, 136).

The belief that tolerance ought to guide human relations led him to record the contribution made to the settlement of Antioquia by two ethnic groups, frequently objects of social discrimination: Negroes and Jews. The controversy over the role of the latter in the settlement of Antioquia (see Chapter 1) did not interest Carrasquilla as a subject of scientific enquiry. The same as Jorge Isaacs, he instinctively leaned toward the controversial theory. Besides, he was puzzled by the vehemence with which the possible Jewish origin had been rejected by some. After all, to belong to the race of Christ, the Rothschilds, Spinoza, and Dreyfus should not be regarded as a major stigma, he observed with a smile (*EPC*, I, 808).

With respect to the Negroes, Carrasquilla's interest and sympathy found concrete expression in character creations which were humanly attractive, displaying not only loyalty but also a strongly developed sense of human dignity. Specific illustrations can be found in "Simon Magus," *Fruits of my Homeland, Hail, Regina, The Marchioness of Yolombó*, and *Long Ago*.

But Carrasquilla went clearly beyond human sympathy and artistic recognition when he demanded flatly that temperament be the determining factor and not the accident of birth. Expanding this postulate, he had harsh words for those who questioned the basic equality of races, defying democracy, death, and the blood of Christ (*EPC*, II, 637).

Carrasquilla's insistence on the golden mean in art extended into the realm of politics. Though raised in the liberal tradition, he recognized merit irrespective of political affiliation. His "Reflections on Berrío" ("Sobre Berrío") offered a splendid tribute to one of the pillars of Colombian conservatism, a man universally revered for his integrity and patriotism and for his sterling personality.

Carrasquilla's psychological and spiritual roots were squarely in the past. When he paused to lament the absence of good humor and spontaneity lost through almighty fashion, it was quite evident that he considered the past superior to the present and that he had little patience with this "period of material positivisms" (*EPC*, I, 749). Modern money worship brought with it a lack of feeling which Carrasquilla deplored openly.

V   *The Role of Religion*

Religion played a significant role in the author's life,[4] convinced as he was that "when a person feels, he is bound to believe" (*EPC*, II, 683). Carrasquilla's capacity for feeling cannot be questioned, and he constantly inquired into problems relating to the sphere "above the roof tops," which defies "fixed rules or human formulae" (*EPC*, I, 598).

From the beginning of his literary career, this genuine interest in the supernatural found expression in colorful stories of Antioqueño folklore endowed with a moral flavor. Francisco Vera ("The Preface of Francisco Vera"—"El prefacio de Francisco Vera"), Doctor Albano ("Cheers"—"Copas"), and Cosme Cruz, (*Ligia Cruz*) undergo more or less abrupt conversions from sinner to saint, while Rogelio and Blanca embody the delicate mystical experience.

Mysticism, that intimate dialogue between humans and their Creator, was thoroughly in tune with Carrasquilla's individualism. He read mystical writings with enthusiasm. Despite this affinity, the author claimed that he was reluctant to write "Blanca" because he felt instinctively that he could not do justice to the delicate experience. The record, in my opinion, proved him wrong. Carrasquilla's ability to capture with equal deftness a gentle spiritual experience and a picaresque religious fraud ("Little Saint Anthony") was a tribute to his creative versatility and his keen gift of obser-

vation. Rogelio and Blanca were doubtless among the most successful of Carrasquilla's literary creatures. Mysticism again entered
the author's thinking in "Balsam for the Spirit" ("Curas de almas")
in describing the dilemma of Father Gil, who was more keenly
conscious of the living temples of the Holy Spirit than of the architectural ones.

The most extensive statement of Carrasquilla's view of religion
is to be found in the novel *Father Casafús*, in which the protagonist,
not unlike Father Gil, is doomed to failure because he raises the
"living temples" over the architectural ones. His crusade against
fanaticism and intolerance brings out clearly the author's common
sense approach, although the extremes of Father Casafús' position
and his inability to compromise point to the practical weaknesses
of the theoretician. In *Father Casafús*, the author came closest to
writing a thesis novel.

Carrasquilla himself was concerned with the "living temples,"
the human essence, and pleaded for a liberal dose of flexibility in
regard to formal ritual. He was critical of those who violated the
essential spirit of religion, and noted that Holy Mass, First Communion, and Holy Week ceremonies in Bogotá were often little
more than dismal farces, with shallow vanity driving out the spiritual
essence. Mass, observed Carrasquilla, has become a rendezvous for
distinguished ladies, where the caprice of fashion and the incentive
of luxury are on display. As far as Holy Week in Bogotá was concerned, the capital might well turn into a "bacchanal in the name
and the memory of our Lord Jesus Christ" (*EPC*, II, 785). The same
concern with externals to the exclusion of the essence blinded a
whole village to the fraudulent practices of Damiancito Rada, an
Antioqueño Tartuffe.[5]

On the other hand, the author registered wholehearted approval
and even admiration for those who in the mystical ambient of a
house, or the retreat of a cell, achieved spiritual communion. Regina
(Hail, Regina), in the midst of majestic nature, worshipped more
effectively standing next to the La Blanca waterfalls than if she were
surrounded by solemn ritual. María Engracia ("The Plant"—"La
mata") experienced a spiritual rebirth, and Margarita Alba ("Mystic
Ecstasy"—"Alma"), one of those "souls which pass through life without anyone being aware of them" (*EPC*, II, 591), reflected the full
potential of that bond of love between God and His creatures.

It is worth noting however that, while raising spiritual essence over ritual form, Carrasquilla was never loath to capture ritual itself in colorful detail. So deeply engrossed could he become in the portrayal of a procession, that he went as far as apologizing, in *The Blue-eyed Boy,* for a particularly lengthy descriptive digression.

The literary career which had begun with the playful atheism of the boy who plunged into space ("Simon Magus") ended in the serene valedictory of the old man "unruffled by the upsets of the present . . . who knows that, beyond this topsy-turvy world, there is the infinite kingdom of the souls, there is Christ" (*EPC*, II, 560).

Religion, then, did not in any way pass unnoticed in his life, even though the prickly exterior and the caustic mask of the sceptic often succeeded in covering up the "true Carrasquilla."[6] The flexibility which he recommended in matters of formal ritual precluded his practicing Roman Catholicism, and his concern with the "living temples" made him lean toward those ethical precepts which are common to all religions.

Mysticism attracted him not only because he was convinced that the "heart needs faith and mystery," but particularly because he insisted that spirituality must issue in positive action. "Praying to God and striking with the mallet" was a pattern of conduct which Carrasquilla wholeheartedly endorsed.[7]

A longing for literary simplicity and a passion for truth pervaded his life. Three essays, "Simplicity in Life," "Simplicity in Science" and "Simplicity in Art," testified to his conviction that simplicity was the essential prerequisite for genuine elegance and that the immortality of Greece in the sphere of the arts remained a lasting tribute to "the simple."

To seek the golden mean was the literary postulate of the man who, in his personal life, did anything but avoid extremes. Consistency, he once remarked, reminded him of a crystal—clear and beautiful, but the image of death (*EPC*, II, 761). Carrasquilla, quite frankly, preferred life with its contradictions.

CHAPTER 3

An Aesthetic Formula

C ARRASQUILLA, said Federico de Onís, was the extraordinary example of a man who became a writer "simply because he could not do otherwise."[1] Literature was the mainspring of his existence and the most potent stimulus all throughout his life. "I who understand life without true love," he confessed in a letter in 1898, "perhaps would not understand it without books" (*EPC*, II, 755). This "innate literary vocation" came close to being an obsession in the life of the man whose creations so frequently were governed by single all-embracing ideas. The statement "I truly love that lady" defined eloquently his intimate relationship to art.

It is difficult therefore to accept the view that "literary comments were of no importance to him."[2] His works show, on the contrary, an abiding concern with such comments. He not only sprinkled them liberally throughout his writings and expounded them with his usual authoritative candor during nocturnal gatherings in the Bastille tavern and other similar establishments, but also set them down in such critical essays as "Homilies" ("Homilías"), "Heresies" ("Herejías"), "Three Names" ("Tres nombres"), "Hackneyed Subject" ("Tema trillado"), "About a Book" ("Sobre un libro"), and "In Defense of the Poet" ("Por el poeta"). Literature occupied him creatively and preoccupied him theoretically. No wonder, then, that he outlined his ideas on its essential nature, striving for an aesthetic formula.

I *Poetry*

Verse clearly was not his medium. The same as Cervantes, he might have lamented that the "Heavens had denied him the poet's grace."[3] Only once did he venture into the foothills of Mount Parnassus, and the resulting sonnet, a sincere tribute to Laura Montoya,[4] did not satisfy the severe autocritic. He later referred to "Salutaris Hostia" as a sin which he "never ever" would commit again. In fact, with the exception of inconsequential *pièces d'occasion*, there is no record of his having broken the weighty promise.

Yet while incapable of writing inspired verse, he took great pains to define his views on poetry with frankness and vigor. Scrutinizing, in the two "Homilies," the *modernista* movement "in relation to Colombian Letters and particularly those of Antioquia" (*EPC*, II, 664), he stated his basic premise that any literary movement must spring organically from a country's cultural life. His classical thesis that "true elegance lies in simplicity" (*EPC*, I, 734) caused him to lash out against artificiality and to berate bitterly those poets who communicated with the select few only. He had absolutely no use for this "horde of savages," who deliberately concealed rather than revealed and who failed to provide a bond of beauty among men.

Carrasquilla may actually have been more in sympathy with certain aspects of the new movement than he himself realized. He acknowledged with some enthusiasm the Parnassian approach to poetry, because of its transparent simplicity. "Who can help being delighted by Sully Prudhomme, Lecomte de Lisle, and Coppée," he declared (*EPC*, II, 667); and he recognized the validity of new techniques to broaden existing poetic horizons. He was far too conscious of the "universality of music" (which he underlined in the second "Homily" and to which, on another occasion, he referred as something in the nature of a "religious cult") to be blind to its literary possibilities. Carrasquilla's negative critical reaction, it would seem, was prompted largely by external phenomena of the local scene, as well as by matters of personalities. Besides, he resented the extreme manifestations of the new school because he feared their limiting effect in terms of public appeal.

Concerned with the sincerity of feeling and its literary reflection, Carrasquilla was disturbed by what he regarded as mere technical skill—*littérature* was the word which Verlaine used scathingly. He categorically rejected any virtuoso performance which was devoid of genuine human feeling. He never ceased to plead with local poets to shun affectation and artificiality, abandon the ivory tower of false emotion, and remain true to their native genius by singing the "hymn of real life" (*EPC*, II, 672).

Firmly convinced that the Parisian brand of decadentism could not thrive on Colombian soil, Carrasquilla cited as the only exception (which in his opinion confirmed the rule) the case of Guillermo

Valencia, suggesting at the same time that the interpretation of his native land would have added an enriching new dimension to Valencia's poetic work. "Remember, triumphant bard" Carrasquilla exclaimed, "that you are a fellow countryman of Jorge Isaacs" (*EPC*, II, 671).

The nationalistic flavor of these recommendations, described with mock humility as "hypothesis rather than thesis," coupled with the categorical way in which they were presented, did not remain unanswered for long. The spokesman for the young *modernistas* was Max Grillo who had come in for particular criticism because of tendencies that Carrasquilla censured as foreign to his native genius. Grillo's spirited defense of the new school in the name of all-powerful change—"everything changes, everything is transformed in every moment which passes"[5] (reminiscent of Sarmiento's impassioned plea that organic growth in language not be curbed)—brought forth Carrasquilla's rejoinder in the form of a "Second Homily." Addressing himself personally to Grillo, he reaffirmed his position that "sincerity and reality" must determine the lasting value of a work of literature and that any poem which is not based on sincerity of feeling cannot be saved by dazzling musical effects. Hermetic poets, Carrasquilla held, besides being frequently lacking in sincerity, were negligent in their task of communicating. "A poet," mused Carrasquilla, "is a traveler who wanders through the world which he alone knows: mankind is entitled to the notes of his journey" (*EPC*, II, 678). In the light of this doctrine, abstruseness cannot be condoned.

Carrasquilla questioned the validity of imitation. There were distinct echoes of Feijoo's doctrine of originality[6] in Carrasquilla's rhetorical question: "What is one writer going to teach . . . another?" (*EPC*, II, 679). His emphatic answer was: Nothing. Ideas are common property and subject to copying. Yet a person's distinctive literary genius is summed up in his style, and imitation in that area is doomed. "Always be Max Grillo" he admonished his friend, "that Grillo who sings of the jungle and the Magdalen River" (*EPC*, II, 682).

Modern reality and sincerity of feeling emerged as his chief criteria. Such a doctrine of course eliminated foreign themes and techniques: "When Grillo 'degrills' himself," Carrasquilla stated unequivocally (*EPC*, II, 768), "he degrades himself."[7]

This emphasis on things native led him, in another critical essay, to exalt a trinity of Antioqueño names which for him represented an inseparable unity—namely, Gregorio Gutiérrez González, Epifanio Mejía, and Juan de Dios Uribe.[8] The "Scientific Report on the Cultivation of Corn in the Hot Climates of the State of Antioquia" ("Memoria científica sobre el cultivo del maíz en los climas cálidos del estado de Antioquia"), a nineteenth century epic by Gutiérrez González, appealed to Carrasquilla because of the harmony between theme, artistic purpose, and poetic expression. The very spontaneity of its cadences, its lack of polish, and its virile spirit turned it into the "epic of our fighting race" (*EPC*, II, 690). Gregorio Gutiérrez González, Carrasquilla noted with approval, remained true to himself and to his milieu.

Epifanio Mejía, whom Carrasquilla called "Gutiérrez González' first born, perhaps his only born" (*EPC*, II, 690), revered nature and his native region, making up for dearth of ideas by an abundance of sincere feeling.[9]

As far as the "third name" was concerned, Uribe dazzled Carrasquilla with his prose style and the eternally youthful enthusiasm of his spirit. Though the critic in this case was doubtless carried away by his own enthusiasm in placing "the Indian" above all other contemporary prose writers,[10] the extreme eulogy served to throw into relief the supreme importance that Carrasquilla was prepared to give to matters of style. Depth of thought was not one of Uribe's strong points, resembling in this respect the poets Gutiérrez González and Epifanio Mejía. Thought was clearly secondary in Carrasquilla's aesthetic scale of values. Art is anything, he proclaimed in a prologue to a volume of verse, as long as it is "truly felt and tastefully treated."[11]

The Colombian poet José Asunción Silva apparently qualified on both counts. Carrasquilla attributed his triumph to the deceptive simplicity of his art and to the universal message of his verse, meaningful to the novice as well as to the expert.

Yet all too many other poets he found wanting in both spontaneity and sincerity. Endowed with learning and fully conversant with "the rules," they lacked nonetheless that basic je ne sais quoi and failed to discharge what Carrasquilla considered their foremost duty, that of communicating.

II *Drama*

The same as poetry, the stage evoked no more than his academic interest. If the sonnet "Salutaris Hostia" remained his solitary attempt to invade the precincts of Mount Parnassus, the effort to "benavent a bit"[12] apparently met with equally dubious success. According to one of the favorite anecdotes in Medellín's literary circles—there is no written record of this episode—Carrasquilla tore up the manuscript of his one and only play when he discovered that the five characters had turned out to be "five Carrasquillas," a further indication of the "eternal delight of autobiography" which injects such a personal flavor into all his writings.

But stagecraft nonetheless held a great charm for him: he was an enthusiastic theatergoer and a keen critic. His comments on the theater and individual performances were prompted chiefly by the visit to Antioquia of the Mexican actress Virginia Fábregas. Carrasquilla's reviews underscored his love for the theater, to which he assigned a key role in human relations. His personal tribute to Virginia Fábregas, a "benefactress missionary" who stilled the spiritual hunger of the public, was genuine and enthusiastic.

Yet his reviews did not add substantially new material to the aforementioned critical comments on poetry. Sincerity and simplicity emerged as basic virtues conducive to a good play and an effective performance. As far as the moral side was concerned—and this question arose in connection with charges of immorality leveled against a play by Berton and Simon—Carrasquilla, like Northrop Frye,[13] rejected any such label as irrelevant. The play, he said, reflected "neither Heaven nor Hell": it portrayed the world. For Carrasquilla it was the spectator whose individual approach determined the morality of the play.[14]

One review deserves special mention because it did add a significantly new note to earlier statements. Carrasquilla commended Emilio Franco's play *If Dogs Could Speak (Si hablaran los perros)* for exploring the hidden recesses of the human spirit, subordinating physical action to psychological activity. This review of a minor work in terms of literary endeavor shed a significant light on Carrasquilla's own creative genius, which assigned a more prominent place to character than to details of the plot.

III   *Prose*

This brings us logically to Carrasquilla's concepts on prose writing and the extent to which he implemented his theories. Very early in his literary career, in the year following *Fruits of my Homeland*, the publication of Eduardo Zuleta's novel *Virgin Soil (Tierra virgen)* prompted not only a searching analysis of the work itself, but a general discussion of the novel genre.[15] Carrasquilla's definition of what constitutes a novel was comfortably broad. "The novel is a piece of life," he observed, "reflected in a writer by means of a heart and a head" (*EPC*, II, 630). This formula provided a spacious enough receptacle to accommodate virtually everything, except "a lie."[16] Truth and beauty remained his indispensable prerequisites for any work of art.

Zuleta's novel received Carrasquilla's nod of approval because it was a slice of life with human psychology as its focal point. The plot was subordinate to the portrayal of character—a book loose in structure, with the protagonist, Manuelito Jácome, providing the unifying element.

Carrasquilla's remarks in this essay foreshadowed some of the salient criteria of his own novelistic technique: the lack of plot, the emphasis on real life, the concern with the individual, the sincerity of feeling.

How about the style, the author's "very own" possession? Here too "Heresies" offered some revealing comments. Starting from the premise that the artist cannot improve on nature since the latter is more beautiful than art, Carrasquilla insisted that nature be imitated as closely as possible. This implied the faithful reproduction of the spoken word, so that the novel would reflect the "very essence of a people or a certain region" (*EPC*, II, 635). The literary work, which, like Zuleta's novel, combined flavorful authentic dialogue with pure narrative prose, offered, in Carrasquilla's view, the greatest variety and aesthetic enjoyment.

The "Second Homily" contained further pertinent references to Carrasquilla's literary taste and aesthetic ideas. Russian literature attracted him with its simplicity and because of its aesthetic concern with the common man rather than with the aristocracy. Nietzsche's emphasis on spontaneity and individual taste as the basis of human liberty struck him as a revitalizing force. Carrasquilla's admiration for Unamuno was based on the latter's sincerity, his dislike for the conventional, and his stress on originality.[17] Some thirty years later, Carrasquilla was to echo this concept in cautioning a fellow novelist, Bernardo Arias Trujillo, against following foreign models (*EPC*, II, 809).

He gave high praise to Francisco Villa López' *Book of Gabriel Jaime (El libro de Gabriel Jaime)*, terming it an "exquisite product."[18] Though being autobiographical, he found it devoid of vanity, copying from nature without exaggerating or idealizing. In a few words of prologue (which appeared first in a letter to Sofía Ospina de Navarro, author of the volume *Tales and Chronicles—Cuentos y crónicas*) Carrasquilla reaffirmed his belief in the supremacy of style. In fact, he regarded style as supreme to such an extent that "the discovery of America badly told is of less artistic value than the faithful description of a mangy dog" (*EPC*, II, 758)—a theory which brings within the novelist's focus "everyday and commonplace events" as long as they are sincerely felt and artistically treated. (The genesis of *Fruits of my Homeland* and the discussion, in "The Literary Casino," of Antioquia's "novelistic milieu" are relevant here.)[19]

On the other hand, a book by Santiago Pérez Triana[20] which had been favorably received by the public did not appeal to Carrasquilla because the author's emphasis was more on philosophy than on description; "He does not feel nature," was Carrasquilla's complaint. Another book was censured by him because the author dwelled on its thesis, "in my view more than a slight defect" (*EPC*, II, 770).

The caustic comments with which Carrasquilla portrayed the literary elite of Bogotá, pointing to the frequent abyss between a literary creation and its author's personality, revealed keen observation and succinct description. Yet, if he was severe with others, he was equally so with himself. Such self-appraisals as "I shall never be a writer" (*EPC*, II, 754) and "Nothing of what I have published seems good to me with the exception of *Hail, Regina*" (*EPC*, I, xxvi) were examples of his autocriticism. A more extreme example can be found in the "Second Homily," where he referred to his own creative endeavors as a "handful of rubbish" (*EPC*, II, 689). Carrasquilla explained the severity of his literary views (with respect to others and to himself) by the wide extent of his readings and his familiarity with the great authors, which combined to fashion his mature aesthetic criterion—a "lofty concept of art" (*EPC*, I, xxvi).

Summing up, then, Carrasquilla's aesthetic formula, his taste was classic, though not without romantic overtones, particularly where the "perpetual delight" of autobiography was involved. Rejecting a thesis as inimical to art, he upheld the importance of exclusive aesthetic orientation. He was more concerned with human nature than with the externals of plot. He regarded a psychologically interesting person as a more lasting source of aesthetic enjoyment than a story chock-full of colorful events. Description, action, and speech must combine harmoniously to bring the character to life. The "everyday and the commonplace" struck him as the most fitting theme because humble happenings of humble people in a humble environment reflected nature at its most spontaneous best. His aesthetic ideal was a national work with modern information, genuine in feeling and sincere in literary treatment; he was uncompromising in pursuing this goal.

In 1898 he lamented that, if he thought and wrote in accordance with his personal aesthetics, he clashed with public opinion; "If I adhere to the latter, I clash with myself" (*EPC*, II, 755). On the horns of this dilemma, Carrasquilla did not hesitate to follow the former course of action, oblivious to public reaction. He thus remained true to himself—spontaneous, simple, and sincere.

CHAPTER 4

The Master Storyteller (1890–1905)

I N examining Carrasquilla's creative curve through forty-six years,
it will be the purpose of this chapter and the two following to
examine the major chronological divisions which contain the key to
his artistic growth. Human beings, the focal point in Carrasquilla's
life, were pivotal to his literary world. His creative process as a
writer of prose fiction was linked inseparably to the portrayal of
their emotions and their speech. Essays, sketches of customs, and
chronicles were little more than a picturesque backdrop to the living
human being to whom he felt akin and whom he probed with
evergrowing curiosity and, indeed, artistic maturity all through his
long life.

I *"Simon Magus"*

The short story "Simon Magus" is commonly considered his *coup
d'essai*. It dates from 1890. The only earlier extant piece of writing
is "El Guarzo," which the centennial edition (*EPC*, I, 671–77) assigns to 1877 and describes as a "curious document."[1]

"Simon Magus" apparently was not intended for publication. The
author, who signed it with the anagramatic form of his name, Carlos
Malaquita,[2] claimed to have "scribbled it hurriedly" merely to satisfy
the admission requirements of Medellín's "Literary Casino." The
result was an entertaining story in autobiographical form—the first
of many in the author's career—in which Carrasquilla evoked a
childhood incident which had painful consequences. The protagonist is Fructuosa Rúa ("Frutos" for short), a trusted family factotum
and as black as the ace of spaces. She began her service in the family
as a slave with the boy's grandparents, left the house for a while to
enjoy freedom when Antioquia liberated its slaves, and perhaps
disenchanted with the taste of that "freedom," eventually returned

to the household of her former employers. At the time of the story she is some sixty years old and every fiber of her existence focuses upon the little boy of eight, the "apple of her eye." Her blind, totally uncritical devotion not only champions the boy's concerns within the confines of his own home but goes so far as to lash out against the school teacher who has been bold enough to censure the boy's conduct. Frutos cannot tolerate the slightest suggestion that her idol might be wrong. The boy, as a logical consequence, comes to accept Frutos as the ultimate authority and her word as gospel. His blind faith leads to the incident which narrowly skirts disaster. Nurtured by fantastic stories of witches and enchanters with which Frutos entertains him, his overheated imagination conceives the plan of emulating these supernatural beings by flying off into space. Obsessed with the idea of performing magic deeds, he and a playmate carry out meticulously the ritual which Frutos outlined in elaborate detail. Jumping from the roof of the pigsty, they doubtless would have come to grief, had it not been for a dung heap placed providentially to soften their fall. The boy escapes serious injury almost by a miracle, but this time not even Frutos is able to save him from his father's wrath. Calixto Muñetón, a prominent villager, sums up the moral of the incident in one succinct sentence: "You see, my young friend, anyone who tries to fly too high generally lands in the pigpen" ("Sí, mi amiguito, todo el que quiere volar . . . chupa"—*EPC*, I, 517).

Is "Simon Magus" autobiographical? In spite of the first person narrative, the evidence is not at all conclusive. The story is not fixed in place; there are no eye witnesses extant today, and the family details evidently do not apply to our author, since Carrasquilla only had one sister.

However, this may be idle speculation. Whether or not Carrasquilla actually underwent a similar Peter-Pan-like experience with his friend and childhood companion Francisco de Paula Rendón (as has been suggested) is not really relevant. The vividly told story rings true for any boy of more than average sensitivity whose imagination has been kindled by a person whom he trusts blindly.

Finally, it should be noted that Carrasquilla at the starting point of his career not only tells a story of universal appeal in regional idiom—something he is to repeat many times after—but that he also hints at two significant concepts which are to recur—namely, the role of a mentor in a young person's life and, more important, the stress on the golden mean and moderation: "Anyone who tries to fly too high generally lands in the pigpen."[3]

II   Fruits of my Homeland

A full length novel followed, *Fruits of my Homeland*, the story of two Medellín families, the Alzates and the Escandones. Written to prove that the state of Antioquia can indeed boast of subject matter which is worthy of being treated in novelistic form, the novel shows how humble human beings in an everyday commonplace setting may be driven to their own downfall by all-embracing ideas. Endowed with a warped sense of values, they become blind to an accurate appraisal of their environment and of themselves in relation to this environment. It is these human beings, caught up in single ideas, who, in my view, remain indelibly etched in the reader's mind long after he has put down the novel and long after he has forgotten the linguistic hurdles which it offers to the uninitiated foreigner.

The world of the Alzates is one of sordid positivism and crude vulgarity with no redeeming features. The devotion to material things, which is a deeply rooted family tradition, reaches its extreme stage in Agustín and Filomena. Mutually complementary, she looks after the wholesale, while he attends to the retail end of the family business. His complete lack of scruples and overwhelming greed become manifest when he asks to be left alone with his dead mother and, after everyone has withdrawn out of respect, proceeds to remove the dead woman's shoes and shawl, offering them for sale in his store a week later. Agustín Alzate is so completely wrapped up in his own importance that he does not greet anyone, business associates being his only contacts. His physical surroundings reflect his personality; there is neatness everywhere, "nothing that smells of books" ("nada que huela a libro"—*EPC*, I, 2). His life is ruled by symmetry and cleanliness; his nose seems "constantly dilated as though conscious of bad odors" ("ensanchada a toda hora y como aspirando malos olores"—*EPC*, I, 3).

If Agustín Alzate's business acumen can be explained by his family background, and possibly by a region which is known "for slaving and for holding on to its belongings like a miserly old lady" ("trabajando como una negra, guardando como una vieja avara"—*EPC*, I, 48), his extreme personal repugnance sets him aside from his environment. After their mother's death, Agustín and Filomena easily manoeuver their two sisters, Belarmina and Nieves, out of their legacy and rapidly move ahead on the road of material wealth. Their world is purely external, based on vanity and greed, with a liberal sprinkling of hypocrisy and totally devoid of spiritual values. An overdeveloped sense of self-importance is mixed with a persecution complex, imagined affronts causing friction with the neighbors. When Agustín receives a public whipping at the hands of the son-in-law of the family whom he has consistently annoyed, his world begins to crumble. The attacker accepts his arrest with equanimity, commenting "It serves me right. Why did I soil my whip?" ("Sí, lo merezco . . . He ensuciado mi fuete"—*EPC*, I, 47).

Agustín does not recover from the blows. The psychological impact of the public humiliation is more powerful and more lasting than the actual pain which the whip has inflicted upon him. As he finds himself lying on the pavement, covered with dust, bleeding, his clothes in disarray, a new chapter seems to begin in "King Augustus' " life. All of a sudden that artificial grandeur which has protected him over the years has vanished, bringing him face to face with reality unvarnished. The psychological consequences are far-reaching for this cardboard tyrant whose despotic rule has, for the first time in his life, been called into question. His vital illusion shattered, stripped of his veneer of grandeur, Agustín vainly hatches sinister plots of vengeance. For him, Agustín Alzate, to have been beaten up by that "scum of the earth" is contrary to all laws of the universe. It is that breach of the universal laws which depresses Agustín long after the physical effects of Bengala's beating have worn off. There is no solution for this man who has lost sight of his fellow men, completely wrapped up in the cult of himself. His rise was rapid; his fall is more so. To add insult to injury, the very person who at the beginning of the novel scolds his sister for allowing colored persons to enter the hallowed ground of his bedroom is subjected toward the end to a lengthy lecture on Christian resignation on the part of the negro servant Bernabela. Agustín is indeed a hollow shell. When his throne comes crashing down and his external veneer of neatness fades, he turns into a melancholy "caricature of fallen grandeur" ("caricatura de la grandeza caída"—*EPC*, I, 115).

Agustín's character does not develop. He is hollow from the outset, and hollow he remains. Like Balzac's Grandet and Molière's immortal miser, his universe is defined in purely material terms.

Unlike Dickens' miser, Carrasquilla's Alzate does not admit of change. The man who begins his career by stealing his dead mother's shoes and shawl confesses at the end of the novel that he is unable to fathom the fact that Filomena can have died "despite her riches."

Filomena's character shows greater complexity than that of her brother. (Carrasquilla's most successful character creations are children and women.) Commercially, Filomena is a match for her brother, to such an extent that when Bengala's well-aimed blows demobilize Agustín, she carries on the business alone. But Filomena's universe, unlike that of Agustín, does not end at the cash register. At forty-five, she is seized by a compulsive yearning for matrimony, and her brother's enforced idleness provides an opportunity to satisfy it. The unsuspecting victim is her nephew from Bogotá, César Pinto, who comes to lend a hand in managing the family business. César "comes, sees, and triumphs," proving a genuine Alzate in all but name. His smooth patter lures his middle-aged aunt into his fangs, blinding her to his deception. Filomena provides an easy mark for this consummate impostor who considers himself a "siren wearing trousers" ("se cree él una sirena con pantalones"—*EPC*, I, 73). His love for her goes as far as her bank account. He quickly "exploits the mine" and abandons his wife.

The two sisters who complete the Alzate household in Medellín are foils to the delusions of grandeur of Agustín and Filomena. Essentially, there is little difference between the behavior pattern of Nieves and that of Belarmina. Nieves, physically deformed, submits humbly to bullying, whereas Belarmina constantly threatens to leave the house, but never carries out her threat. Both sisters have lost their independence of action, though Belarmina retains at least a voice of noisy protest.

While the Alzate part of the plot develops on an unattractive plane of reality, the secondary plot of the novel injects romantic flavor, providing a measure of relief from the consistently sordid motivations which inspire the chief protagonists. Besides, there is doubtless autobiography in the character of Martín Gala. The young student, determined to shine among his companions in every respect except in the field of scholastic excellence, brings to mind the apt words of description with which Antonio José Restrepo recalls his old friend Carrasquilla in 1875.[4] Our author may have been thinking of that period in his life when he speaks of Martín Gala as the "greatest heretic which Minerva's religion had" ("el mayor hereje que tuvo la religión de Minerva"—*EPC*, I, 30). Martín's idol is Lord Byron, and he is intent on emulating the crippled English poet to the letter.

This thoroughly unstable young man meets María Josefa Escandón (nicknamed Pepa) under somewhat strange circumstances. The initial ambush and provocation on the part of the vivacious and whimsical daughter of Pacho Escandón triggers a series of chain reactions. Martín, subjected to public ridicule that first Sunday afternoon outside Pepa's house, vows vengeance. A "war of nerves" follows in which Martín's strategy follows a familiar pattern. Goaded by his vanity—like César Pinto, he may have considered himself a "siren in trousers"—he picks up the gauntlet which the girl has thrown to him. He decides to pursue the skirmish until he enamours the girl and, at the first signs of love on Pepa's part, to abandon her. The plan of "vengeance" backfires of course, and Martín soon discovers that he is far from impervious to Pepa's charms. The entertaining battle continues, in keeping with the motto that "all is fair," and both contestants resort occasionally to "disdain to fight disdain." Finally, Martín crumbles under the emotional strain. At that critical juncture in their relations, and faced with a complete nervous breakdown in "irresistible" Martín, the coquettish young lady decides that the game has gone far enough. Her capitulation shows that, the same as Martín, proud Pepa has not been able to play the game with impunity and that the girl who prided herself on being immune to love has succumbed.

Pepa is a delightful novelistic creation, whimsical, coquettish, the despair of her parents, and endowed with a contagious laugh which "injects the microbes of happiness into everyone" ("inoculaba a todo el mundo los microbios del regocijo"—EPC, I, 37). Don Pacho, her wealthy father, is graced with a crude tongue. In fact, we are told that when people in Medellín wished to emphasize the fact that something was unusually dirty they would say: "It is filthier than Pacho Escandón's mouth" ("Es más sucia que la boca de don Pacho Escandón"—EPC, I, 91). His favorite habit reached such a degree that the priest at confession time exacted from him a promise to watch his language. Apparently Escandón was so depressed as a result of this vow that the priest was persuaded to lift the ban.

Besides contradicting others, Escandón likes nothing better than to "shock the bourgeois," particularly his wife. But all this verbal display is really nothing more than a pose, since underneath it all he is not only a worthy citizen but also decency and rectitude itself.

Like Belarmina Alzate, Don Pacho's bark is worse than his bite, and his resistance to the marriage of Pepa and Martín is more vocal than real. Part of his noisy objection is the result of his close bond with his daughter and an instinctive unwillingness to share her affection with anyone. Possessiveness is at the root of his actions, and his crude mask disguises genuine tenderness.

Fruits of my Homeland is not a psychological novel. It does not probe the mind or heart, nor does it make an attempt to delve into human relationships. Carrasquilla, while copying from life and displaying keen observation and deft powers of description, as well as an expert knowledge of his milieu, remains on the outside of his characters. There is no development of character, and the "novelistic subject matter" does not go past the picturesque exteriors. The lack of human depth in his first full length novel does not prepare the reader for the sensitive psychological studies which he will encounter in Carrasquilla's later writings. The author's domain here at the outset of his career is "repulsive reality" coupled with unbridled romanticism. The result is, Carrasquilla claims in his "Autobiography," the "first prosaic novel which has been written in Colombia . . . without in the slightest idealizing the reality of life" ("la primera novela prosaica que se ha escrito en Colombia . . . sin idealizar en nada la realidad de la vida"—*EPC*, I, xxvi).[5] Despite their human variety, Carrasquilla's five principal characters have one trait in common. They are asocial creatures to a greater or lesser degree, propelled by the almighty ego and suffering from an overdeveloped sense of self-importance.

The division into two separate plots, only tenuously related by the scene of events, is questionable as a structural device. Out of the thirty chapters of the novel, seventeen are concerned with the rise and fall of "King Augustus" and "Queen Filomena" and with César's unsavory triumph, whereas thirteen deal with the entertaining details of Martín Gala's courtship, brief fall (when Pepa derides him publicly), and subsequent rise. The plots develop in alternating chapters without connecting link until Chapter XXIII, where the rhythm is suspended and the Alzate plot takes precedence, with the final eight chapters being entirely devoted to it. It is not easy to see why the author decided to separate the two aspects of the plot so completely, except by pointing out that there is really no connection between the Alzates and the Escandones. Their two worlds never meet, and there is only one passing ref-

erence during the wedding festivities of Pepa and Martín to the fact
that "another loving couple" has departed happily for Bogotá on
their honeymoon.

Carrasquilla himself defends the double plot structure, not only
by citing the ambitious example of *War and Peace*,[6] but also by
suggesting that complexity of plot and character is after all an integral part of the novel genre. Besides, he must have felt that the
unbridled romanticism of Martín and Pepa provides a refreshing
counterbalance to the untrammeled materialism of the "unholy trinity" of Agustín-Filomena-César. That, to me, is the most likely
reason for coupling two entirely independent narratives which easily
could have resulted in two separate books.

Both plots were utilized separately by the novelist's sister, Isabel
Carrasquilla de Arango, for her two dramatizations, *Filo y Sarito*
and *Pepa Escandón;*[7] while Enrique de la Casa's adaptation of the
novel under the title *Tipos colombianos* (Salt Lake City, 1948) ignores Pepa and Martín, concentrating on the Alzate family. In the
prologue to the first edition (Bogotá, 1896), Pedro Nel Ospina describes Martín's sentimental entanglements as "inferior to the rest,"
and the Spanish novelist José María de Pereda modifies his generally
complimentary comments by observing that "what is not
Alzate . . . almost disturbs in the novel."[8] Apparently there were
some who after seeing the novel in manuscript form voiced the
extreme view that it was "little less than detestable" (*EPC*, I, xxvi),
thinking no doubt of the "rotten fruit" which Carrasquilla chose to
portray.

In sum, the elements which stand out in *Fruits of my Homeland*
are the picturesque regional milieu and the mastery of style, showing the author equally at home in literary language and in the
vernacular. But altogether, and notwithstanding the bold claim
which Carrasquilla makes in his "Autobiography," the novelist
clearly is not yet at ease in the novel genre. Antonio Curcio Altamar's
reservation is a valid one: *Fruits of my Homeland* suffers from a
distinct "lack of nuances."[9] Above all Carrasquilla falls short in his
portrayal of human nature, which later on was to become one of his
most remarkable assets as a novelist.

III   *"In the Right Hand of the Father"*

1897 witnessed the publication of three of Carrasquilla's works,
"In the Right Hand of the Father," "Blanca," and *Dimitas Arias*,

the first two short stories, the last a short novel. A letter to Max Grillo, dated April 21, 1898, provides some details about the genesis of the first, going back to the sixties, when our author listened to the story for the first time in the El Criadero mines. Carrasquilla claims to have heard the story again in the eighties, told this time by Teresa Roldán, a vendor of foodstuffs. So impressed was he with the subject, the picturesque setting, and the characters that when he was asked to write a folk tale, he preferred the Peralta theme over other popular favorites. The result was the first tale of the collection *Above the Roof Tops (De tejas arriba)*, universally acclaimed as the finest of that group.

The outline of the story is simple enough and has familiar overtones: A poor man who continually gives aid to those more wretched than himself is granted five wishes to reward his charity and integrity. Peralta's choices, which perplex his supernatural visitors by their blending of ingenuousness and astuteness, soon lead to problems. Not only does the shrewd Antioqueño peasant confound all his opponents at the card table, but he promptly forces death to "take a holiday," causing disastrous effects of "unemployment" in heaven and in hell.

Slightly less than half the story depicts a delightful Antioqueño vision of the hereafter, with playful echoes of Dante's *Divine Comedy* and Quevedo's *Dreams*. Peralta, having departed from this earth, proceeds with the same carefree attitude as before. Invading the precincts of hell, and conscious of his magic gift, he challenges the devil to a card game in which he wins well over thirty-three thousand million souls. Yet such legitimate spoils raise the theological problem of what to do with all those lost souls which Peralta's *tute*[10] skill has retrieved. After disposing of the problem with the expert counsel of Saint Theresa and Saint Thomas, Peralta uses the one and only remaining wish with considerable wisdom:

growing tinier and tinier until he had turned into a three inch Peralta and forthwith, with the nimbleness which is given to the blessed, he lept into the world which the Father holds in His right hand. He made himself thoroughly at home and embraced the cross. There he remains for all eternity. (se fue achiquitando, achiquitando hasta volverse un Peraltica de tres pulgadas, y derechito, con la agilidá que tienen los bienaventuraos, se brincó al mundo que tiene el Padre en su diestra. Se acomodó muy bien y se abrazó con la cruz. Allí está por toda la eternidá.) *EPC*, I, 528

Carrasquilla termed it simply "a folklore which depicts our peo-

ple." Indeed there is a delightful human and intimately local quality
about the whole story, altogether a flavor which the author was not
to equal again. The human material is of genuine Antioqueño peasant stock. Peralta is practical, hard-headed, soft-hearted, endowed
with a sound dose of commonsense and a liberal sprinkling of picaresque astuteness. He is unconcerned and by and large unruffled
(the two key words which the author uses time and again to describe
his hero are *desentendido* and *parejo*). He does not worry about the
future either on earth or in the hereafter. Having been unconcerned
with asking for paradise when Jesus offers him five wishes, he remains unconcerned for the remainder of his life. After death, he
moves along "with the carefree attitude of his whole life" (*EPC*, I,
524). There is a curious parallel between the great scoffer of Seville[11]
and the unruffled little man called Peralta. Both are only concerned
with what lies immediately ahead, supremely confident that the
long-range future will take care of itself. Meanwhile Peralta does
good. (At this point, of course, the analogy ends.)

The story is richly endowed with boisterous humor, not a common
commodity in the literary panorama of a continent which on the
whole tends to be on the gloomy side. It is truly a work which is
"spoken rather than written." Carrasquilla evidently enjoys himself
tremendously in telling the tale and reproducing as closely as possible the picturesque speech of his fellow countrymen.

A few typical examples must suffice to show the master storyteller
at his best. Who can forget such uproarious glimpses as the royal
couple feasting on hot chocolate, biscuits, and fresh cheese and
inviting Peralta to take his place between them (*EPC*, I, 522); or
Saint Peter scratching his bald pate, grunting, and in exasperation
pulling Peralta by his *ruana*[12] to steer his unorthodox wishes in a
heavenly direction (*EPC*, I, 520); or death (who has come to take
Peralta away) demonstrating his agility by jumping on the pronged
branch of an avocado tree to which he promptly remains glued;[13]
or the devil, who, affected by this involuntary holiday in heaven
and in hell like so many others, has decided to kill time curing his
itch and ends up playing *tute* with Peralta and losing an inflationary
number of souls. No less delightful is the ingenious solution to a
knotty theological problem, sponsored by Saint Thomas and Saint
Theresa, which explains evil on earth in perpetuity and precipitates
Peralta's jump into the glorious "right hand of the Father." There
are many other equally unforgettable moments which show the
blend of an incongruous situation and charmingly local color. Per-

haps, as has been suggested, the only adequate comment on the author's style in this instance would be to copy the story in its entirety. Carrasquilla ironically referred to a supposed "French original," which no one had been able to discover.[14] Some thirty years later, the Argentine novelist Ricardo Güiraldes incorporated into his novel *Don Segundo Sombra* a similar folk tale in gaucho attire. Güiraldes' variation on the popular theme of course did not derive from Carrasquilla. In fact, the Argentine version, which makes use of the device of wishes to reward charity (the same as does Carrasquilla) is more closely related to "Nonna Miseria," one of the tales of *Le novelline di Santo Stefano* (1869) collected by Angelo de Gubernatis.[15] Both the Italian and Argentine versions resort to a person's name to explain the presence of misery in the world. The basic difference is that, while the Italian tale centers around a destitute old woman named Misery, Güiraldes' hero is a struggling blacksmith by that name. Carrasquilla's story of Peralta bears but a superficial resemblance in theme to either. His sovereign pen and riotous imagination fashioned an autonomous masterpiece.[16]

IV *"Blanca"*

While Carrasquilla was unusually enthusiastic about "In the Right Hand of the Father," he was less than lukewarm about the story "Blanca." Max Grillo apparently liked it, and the Antioqueño reading public at large seems to have placed it on a level with Samuel Velásquez' novel *Mother (Madre)*, which appeared in Medellín in the same year as "Blanca." Carrasquilla himself termed it "pretty bad and insignificant" (*EPC*, II, 755), insisting that the delicate candor of the subject was alien to his artistic temperament.

As the story opens, we find the child heroine busily erecting a statue of the Virgin. The magnum opus, executed with the most intense concentration, bears "the nonsensical stamp of infantile aesthetics" (*EPC*, I, 529). Having completed her masterpiece on top of a box and making use, for its adornment, of materials which she has gathered all around the house, the little girl gets to her knees to improvise the sanctification ceremony. The string of prayers which bubbles forth from those little lips is so completely original, not to say incoherent, that the author conjectures only Mary may be able to capture its full meaning.

This charming first scene of the story is the key to what follows.

Blanca is a precocious, hypersensitive girl who has always preferred nature to playing with dolls and whose magnificent obsession is the Virgin Mary. Everyone in the family worships the child, with the exception of her own father, Alberto Rivas, who is more concerned with pleasure than with moral values and who prefers outside entertainment to family life. Her mother, Ester, bears her cross heroically, clinging to Blanca and showering upon the child all the affection which her husband does not value. When Alberto suffers a bicycle accident and is confined to bed, Ester does not shirk her duty. "There began one of those unconscious vengeances of the loving and self-denying wife, of the Antioqueño woman, whose talents are in her heart" ("Principió una de esas venganzas inconscientes de la esposa amante y abnegada, de la mujer antioqueña, que tiene el talento en el corazón"—*EPC*, I, 534), and little Blanca loyally helps in this "vengeance," spelling her mother in dancing attendance on the patient. And the miracle happens: that bout of sickness and the subsequent convalescence period gradually cement the broken home, restoring the marital relationship. When his friends stay away after the one and only visit prompted by duty, Alberto comes to realize little by little the shallow artificiality of those values which for so many years had replaced—so he thought at least—his home life and had prevented him from doing his duty as husband and father. With Alberto's change of heart, marital harmony returns to the Rivas home, a development which Ester attributes entirely to Blanca's ministry.

The family seems to have reached the "zenith of happiness" (*EPC*, I, 537), and the grandfather's birthday should, for a variety of reasons, be a most joyous occasion. Instead it brings disaster. The birds which Blanca has been promised as a reward for her charming poetry recital become identified in her mind with the emissaries of her beloved Virgin. "Will the Virgin send the little birds to the birthday party?" is all she can think while the preparations progress in the house. In the midst of the party, Blanca suddenly spies a humming bird in the garden which to her heralds the arrival of the winged visitors. Very much like the two boys in "Simon Magus" who choose to defy the law of gravity with near-disastrous consequences, Blanca steals away from the crowd to pursue her ideal and drowns in the pond. When the horrified family rushes to the scene, her white hat floats on the surface of the water "like an enormous daisy" (*EPC*, I, 540).

One might well criticize the denouement for being too brusque. It contrasts sharply with the festive atmosphere of the birthday party. Yet there are indications all throughout the story to suggest that happiness is a fleeting thing. Ester cannot resist the forebodings of tragedy, and when disaster strikes, it is all the more painful because it affects the very person who has given enjoyment to most. Blanca dies in pursuit of a dream which has reached obsessive dimensions.

The delicacy of "Blanca" contrasts with both the ugly realities of *Fruits of my Homeland* and the earthy vitality of "In the Right Hand of the Father." The child dazzled by an obsessive dream brings to mind the leitmotif of "Simon Magus" seven years earlier. Otherwise, and except for Blanca herself, there is little psychological interest in any of the characters, with the possible exception of Alberto, whose moral awakening is aided—precipitated according to the mother—by Blanca's ministry.

The story is dedicated to the women of Medellín, whose "talents are in their hearts" (*EPC*, I, 534). Carrasquilla's tribute is doubtless sincere. Ester ushers in an array of female characters in Carrasquilla's writings who usually represent common sense and womanly charm. At the same time, our author is not given to glossing over female weakness. "The Saints even in the Heavens remain women," he remarks in commenting on the saintly ladies' vain attempt to eavesdrop on celestial secrets between the Lord and Saint Peter ("In the Right Hand of the Father"—*EPC*, I, 526).

As in "Simon Magus" and *Fruits of my Homeland*, the weakness of "Blanca" lies in its characters being too much of one piece and too lacking in depth and nuances to be psychologically interesting. The strength of the story once again is in its narrative, which testifies to the author's versatility. I cannot find the story artificial, despite Carrasquilla's personal misgivings. Its spiritual orientation foreshadows "Rogelio," and its delicate single idea is a prelude to the novel *Dimitas Arias*.

V Dimitas Arias

The latter is doubtless a far more ambitious effort than "Blanca." It is the story of a rural schoolmaster, Dimas, a melancholy piece of humanity who has been confined to a wheelchair for thirty years. Dimas' body, we are told, is the size of that of a boy of eight (*EPC*,

I, 544), and his pupils cannot help but marvel how a human head forms part of so tiny a body. Life has been an uninterrupted series of tragedies for poor Dimas. First he is crippled as a result of an accident caused by drunken companions; then his only child dies three days after birth. The cripple vegetates until the village priest takes pity on him and decides to give his useless life a purpose. After a training period of nine months, conducted personally by the priest, Dimas is appointed teacher in a newly opened school in the district. It is there that we meet him at the beginning of the story, struggling vainly from his wheelchair to maintain a semblance of discipline in this "miniature Babel" of unruly children and to impart some knowledge at the same time. His chief qualification for this position is undoubtedly the "sound heart in his sick body" (*EPC*, I, 544). Love for children is thought to make up for severe intellectual and pedagogic shortcomings. The children's cooperation is minimal, and discipline is an unknown quantity in Dimas' classroom, with corporal punishment being the order of the day. Carmen Aguirre and Toto Herrera are the gang leaders. Above all, Carmen is a "holy terror," lazy and obstreperous during school hours while inexplicably the very opposite outside of school—kindness and solicitousness incarnate.

In spite of his daily calvary, Dimas is deeply attached to the delapidated school building because of the contact which it affords him with young people. When progress invades the village and substitutes state institutions and trained personnel for his improvised school, Dimas loses his raison d'être. Deprived of his lifeline, he is nothing but a "body awaiting burial" (*EPC*, I, 559). Physically, he has been leading a shadow existence since the crippling accident had turned him into a permanent invalid. Removed from the schoolroom, his spiritual world begins to crumble, and he becomes keenly conscious of his futility and, above all, of the burden which this futility constitutes for Vicenta, his self-denying wife. This compulsive "childhood nostalgia," which the little schoolhouse has allowed him to satisfy vicariously and which has suddenly been cut short, leads to dejection, delirium, and eventually, mental derangement.

In the twilight of insanity, the frail old man resorts to a pathetic device to escape from his spiritual isolation and to satisfy his overwhelming desire for childhood. His favorite Christ child statue turns into a creature of flesh and blood, becoming identified in his mind with his own son Dimitas whom he had never seen. This "strange madness, delicate in its very extravagance" (*EPC*, I, 560), gives meaning to his wretched life. He refuses to let go of this Dimitas; he caresses and teaches him, though curiously enough he is never concerned with feeding him: "Nothing for his body, everything for his spirit" (*EPC*, I, 560). When the old man will not part with his Dimitas even for a minute, his former pupil, Carmen, whose warm heart had triumphed over her thoughtlessness, resorts to a ruse, slipping a straw puppet into the cripple's hands. In human terms, the substitution really is immaterial. In clinging to what he believes to be his child, Dimas' wretched life has found fulfillment.

The autobiographical flavor in *Dimitas Arias* is pronounced. Carrasquilla himself, in his "Autobiography," refers to "the cripple" who was his first teacher, later the "protagonist of some story of mine" (*EPC*, I, xxv). Since, according to his own confession, he "never learnt anything anywhere," the stimulus with which the village school provided him was no doubt more literary than intellectual.

Samuel Velásquez, author of the novel *Mother*, expressed amazement at Carrasquilla's ability to turn any trifle, any commonplace occurrence, into a subject for a literary creation, even though, as in the case of *Dimitas Arias*, the subject is apparently "insipid, sterile, and dry." This statement needs a word of qualification. While *Dimitas Arias* indeed draws on the ordinary for background and theme, I should nonetheless hesitate to describe it as trivial, insipid, or sterile. The tragedy of the rural "teacher without pupils" who comes to seek spiritual solace in a strange illusion is a deeply moving subject which requires a sensitive pen. The story in its psychological penetration and its human nuances shows a clear advance over the light and playful chatter of "Simon Magus" and the monolithic *Fruits of my Homeland*. The delicate single idea to which the cripple clings continues in a way the obsession which gives delicate meaning to Blanca's young life.

Vicenta, the village priest, and above all young Carmen and Toto, who make Dimas' school days thoroughly miserable but who are the first to rush to his aid when he is in serious straits, are living people drawn from nature. Yet the only character drawn in depth and probed psychologically is the cripple himself—a thoroughly rewarding creation.

It seems that Carrasquilla himself was attracted to this story and to its protagonist. A reference in a letter to Grillo raises *Dimitas*

Arias over "Blanca" because the subject matter, Carrasquilla confesses, strikes a responsive chord in his creative genius (*EPC*, II,
755). We also recall that after paralysis immobilized him in 1928,
he complained to his friend Ignacio Cabo: "All I need to do is open
a school and clutch a Christ Child to be like my hero Dimitas Arias"
(*EPC*, II, 802).

VI   *"The Lonely Soul"*

The year 1898 brought another excursion into folklore and supernatural regions. The protagonist of "The Lonely Soul," scion of
a powerful father of ancient nobility, has everything a man can ask
for. He is the epitome of beauty, intelligence, and moral virtue.
Being the only male heir, his father worships him, and the future
holds the greatest promise in store for the youth in terms of
achievement and fame.

All this is wiped out in one fateful moment through an unfinished
sentence, left dangling after the conjunction "BUT." This slanderous
"BUT," uttered by his favorite teacher Reinaldo (a person as thoroughly trusted by the youth as is Frutos in "Simon Magus"), un-
leashes disaster, sowing dissension, snuffing out a family, hurling
two souls into hell, and "depriving the earth of infinite blessings
and the heavens of infinite Saints" (*EPC*, I, 570). Condemned to
wander through the world to expiate for the dire consequences of
his unfinished sentence, Reinaldo finally is allowed a fleeting
glimpse of what this world might have been, were it not for that
fateful "BUT." Then his slanderous tongue is torn out and deposited
on top of the town pillory. There it remains, defying any attempt
to remove it, "bloody, palpitating, indestructible like calumny" as
a warning symbol (*EPC*, I, 570).

This is one of the few among Carrasquilla's stories which ends on
a distinctly moral note. Coming just one year after the delightful
tale of Peralta, "The Lonely Soul" suffers by comparison. It has
none of the features which turn the former into an immortal masterpiece. It lacks the picturesque speech, the humor, the vibrant
figures both natural and supernatural. The characters are types.
Even the narrative is pedestrian, slow and heavy. Its one redeeming
feature would seem to be its wealth of imagination and variety of
incident, contrasting what might have been with what actually is.
But—and a discussion of "The Lonely Soul" could hardly be com-

plete without a "BUT"—it lacks the light touch. Moral or didactic tales are not Carrasquilla's forte.

VII *"Little Saint Anthony"*

The following year witnessed the publication of two works, one a short story, the other, a short novel. Both of them involve the ticklish question of religious fanaticism, first in the contemporary context, then in historical perspective. Though both seem playful at first sight, they have decidedly serious overtones.

"Little Saint Anthony" can claim everything that "The Lonely Soul" lacks—namely, living people and speech, humor, and a living situation. It is a perfect short story, which holds the reader's interest until the totally unexpected ending. It shows how skillful mass hypnosis of an unscrupulous rogue, coupled with a dose of wishful thinking on the part of sincere and ingenuous people, can lull an entire village into the most extravagant hopes and dreams. Damián Rada, the fifteen year old hero of the story (or should I say the antihero because of his decidedly picaresque attributes?), succeeds in hoodwinking the gullible "evildoers of good" by virtue of meekness and pious demeanor and gentle phrases, all of which he studiously practices at the proper moments and in strategic places so as to be noticed or overheard by the right people.

The boy's unfortunate exterior seems to belie his moral qualities. His figure looks "more like a foetus than like a boy" (*EPC*, I, 572), but his hypnotic personality is so irresistible that even Medellín succumbs to his spell. He is nicknamed "Aguedita's little priest," because the person who started him on his spiritual road is Aguedita Paz, who regards her life as one uninterrupted apostolic dream.

When village charity, mobilized by his chief benefactress and mentor, sends the boy to Medellín to further his studies, Damián is not long in bewitching his new environment with that "inner light" which seems to point to his genuine vocation (*EPC*, I, 573). But above all, the virtuous Del Pino ladies who run a boarding house in Medellín are impressed with the modesty of their new protegé, who demurely lowers his eyes as soon as the attractive maid Candelaria appears on the scene. There is no doubt in their minds: some day the Antioqueño church will have in Damián Rada a second Saint Thomas, provided he does not die before, "because the boy does not seem made for this world" (*EPC*, I, 574).

While one of the sisters is dazzled by his moral virtues, the other takes affectionate charge of his physical needs, endeavoring to strengthen the boy's fragile frame. For two whole years the "little saint" enjoys life to the full, forging signatures, counterfeiting seminary certificates—rumor even had it that he went as far as associating with Protestants (*EPC*, I, 576)—while delighting his gullible benefactresses with his humble, seraphic smile. When the moment of truth comes and the boy vanishes, the ladies' dream world collapses. Damiancito Rada, the Antioqueño Tartuffe, had killed one of their dearest illusions and, in the process, deprived them of an able maid. (Evidently Damián's eyes did not remain permanently lowered!)

I said initially that this is a playful story with serious overtones. The playful element lies in the rascally manoeuvers of a boy who not only plays hookey for two years but who falsifies documents to prolong his "enchanting indolence." The serious overtones concern the relationship between Damián's consummate acting and his benefactresses, whose sincere gullibility encourages his unscrupulous behavior. Carrasquilla's artistic accent, it would seem to me, is not on the boy's irresponsible pranks, but rather on Aguedita Paz and, particularly, on the Del Pino sisters in Medellín.

The tear falling from Fulgencia's eye on the fiber sandal which the boy has left behind tells the tale. A whole world has been shattered by a mischievous little rogue, but there is forgiveness in that final heartfelt tear (*EPC*, I, 577). While the unscrupulous pranks of Damián Rada provide an entertaining twist, the excellence of Antioquia's Tartuffe variant rests on the author's penetrating commentary on those many people in all lands and all social layers who are guided by sincere impulse and emotion rather than by mature reflection. Perhaps Damián thinks too much and his benefactresses too little. Carrasquilla's keen observation creates a fine short story, at once local and universal, in "Little Saint Anthony."

VIII   Father Casafús

The novel *Father Casafús*, entitled originally *Little Luther* (*Luterito*), evolves around a fearless priest who not only insists on speaking his mind but who claims the privilege of following the dictates of his conscience irrespective of social, political, and religious pressures. Totally uncompromising in his crusade against flattery and servility, Pedro Nolasco Casafús is a study in intransigence. The battle lines are drawn in a village setting in Antioquia against the historical background of the war of 1876: on one side, the parish priest Ramón María Vera, endowed with "evangelical simplicity" (*EPC*, I, 144), and a group of parishioners led by "red baiter" Efrén Encinales and Quiteria Rebolledo de Quintana, whom Casafús' frank comments in the confessional have outraged beyond any hope of reconciliation (*EPC*, I, 142–43); on the other, Casafús, backed by his loyal ally Milagros Lobo (nicknamed Milagritos).

There is absolutely no common ground between the blunt nature of Casafús and the disarmingly simple soul of Father Vera. "Father Vera," exclaims Casafús at one point, "you are an imbecile" (*EPC*, I, 154). His branding of the Antioqueño crusade as "Satan's supreme triumph" (*EPC*, I, 160) and his exhortation that parishioners obey the central government bring Casafús' immediate suspension. The stern episcopal reprimand causes soul searching in the village. Has Casafús' "inflammatory" sermon been properly understood?

In the culminating episode of the novel, Milagritos pleads with the bishop of the diocese to temper justice with mercy. Her charming and extremely eloquent intercession produces Casafús' reinstatement and indeed his transfer to another village. Her mission accomplished, she returns, only to learn, thunderstruck, that Casafús died in her absence. The sudden lifting of the ban caused the austere ascete to die—of all things—of "overeating" (*EPC*, I, 174).

At first sight, the abrupt denouement would seem to provide a classic illustration for E. M. Forster's remark that "nearly all novels are feeble at the end."[17] Yet the concluding statement in this novel, anticlimactic as it may appear, is basically in accord with the introductory one. Both hold the key to the hero's character. That quick temper is at the root of all his troubles (*EPC*, I, 141), and at the end, we learn that he gorged himself, with fatal results. Throughout his life, Casafús remains addicted to extremes which turn him into a comic figure. He is curiously reminiscent of Molière's Alceste in *Le Misanthrope*, who also ignores the obvious fact that frankness practiced in excessive doses becomes self-defeating.

Casafús is doomed to fail just as Alceste must fail because both are unable to make concessions to the world around them and refuse to say a saving word. At that point, their effectiveness is lost, and it becomes difficult to take them too seriously.[18]

The situation is complicated by the fact that all the worthy matrons

are sure of the righteousness of their actions and genuinely concerned with protecting the holy faith. Father Vera, neither an intellectual nor a theological giant, does his utmost to see clearly, but
is rebuffed by Casafús. The latter, suggesting that he cannot change
his conscience as he does his cassock and that God is "peace and
under no circumstances war" (*EPC*, I, 162), will not tolerate discussion on what he regards as fundamentals.

With both warring factions fanatically convinced of the validity
of their respective positions, the breakdown in communication becomes inevitable. While Carrasquilla is evidently critical of both
sides, he shows his sympathy for the liberal position, particularly
through that attractive Milagritos, whose memorable intercession
on Casafús' behalf provides a climactic moment in the novel.[19]

Father Casafús occupies a unique position in Carrasquilla's creative work. In tackling the problem of religious fanaticism and political intrigue in rural districts (*EPC*, I, 173), Carrasquilla comes
closer to expounding a thesis than either before or after. Preaching,
indeed, was not his forte, although in one of his letters from the
mine he referred to himself caustically as the parish priest of San
Andrés. He was critical of León Varney's book for emphasizing a
thesis, "not a very slight defect in my view" (*EPC*, II, 770). Yet,
in *Father Casafús*, Carrasquilla, not unlike Galdós in *Doña Perfecta*
and *Gloria*, lashes out against fanaticism and intolerance wherever
they might occur and shows how uncompromising extremes may
well defeat a fundamentally sound position.

IX   *"Money Talks"*

The short story "Money Talks" ("¡A la plata!") focuses on the poor
peasant class. The author, in his introductory paragraph, describes
the human setting as something which seen from above looks very
much like a garbage dump (*EPC*, I, 578), exhaling the genuine
stench of humanity. It is fair day in the village, and the motley
crowd, partaking of the most varied refreshments, offers a picture
of lively animation. However, the carefree mood changes abruptly
to one of panic when, without warning, a detachment of twenty
soldiers bursts upon the square, gathering all able-bodied men for
military service in the "Thousand Days" civil war. One single word,
encierro ("we're trapped"), on everyone's lips, sums up the relentless human roundup which ensues: it carries all the ominous weight

of a "prelude to the final judgment" (*EPC*, I, 578). For Longas it is indeed final. Hiding in the church is of no avail; neither is the tearful intervention of his daughter, María Eduvigis. He remains among the human prey and must take his leave with the others (*EPC*, I, 578). Longas' parting words are addressed to his wife and to his daughter; a word of instruction regarding work to the former, a word of caution concerning off duty hours to the latter: "Beware of the boss!" (*EPC*, I, 579).

Longas' departure "to the wars" seems to make a deeper impression on the beautiful and somewhat coquettish Eduvigis than on her mother Rufa. Rufa adjusts easily to separation, just as easily as she has adjusted to her two sons' imprisonment, and does not waste too much time lamenting her husband's absence. The very antithesis to loyal self-denying Ester (in "Blanca"), Rufa demonstrates the fact that "sentimentalities of the heart are . . . a superfluous luxury for the poor peasant" (*EPC*, I, 580). Rufa's latest pastime, which completely absorbs her attention, is panning gold. She is a businesswoman from head to foot, hardheaded and practical, devoid of sentimentality of any kind. When the conscript returns one fine day, looking no less grotesque than when he departed, he discovers to his dismay that his daughter has heeded his words of caution to the letter. Unfortunately, while forewarned about the intentions of the wealthy boss, she was taken unawares by penniless Simplicio. Longas feels crushed by "dishonor" when it dawns upon him that the father of the chubby baby that he picked up with grandfatherly pride just a moment before does not have a cent to his name.

The story emphasizes authentic regional detail as well as habits of speech. (When Longas speaks, for example, he does so in the typical manner "of the native peasant of our easterly region"—*EPC*, I, 579). It comes close to being naturalistic in its unrelenting emphasis on the ugly, unfeeling, and calculating. The first glimpse the reader catches is that of the human refuse pile, complete with a variety of stench. The three main characters on whom the novelist's lens focuses eventually appear to be worthy exponents of that refuse pile. They are totally devoid of human emotion—a luxury, says Rufa, which only the upper class can afford. "Money Talks" is well told, but humanly, it is too grotesquely extreme to be convincing. Its denouement is consistent with an atmosphere in which the dance of gold rules supreme.

The story was composed to comply with the ground rules of a

literary contest which laid down both subject matter and length of the piece. Carrasquilla's artistic temperament must have rebeled instinctively against the restraining fact of being commissioned. This might help to account for the evident flaws which mar the story.

X   Hail, Regina

Hail, Regina was another commissioned piece. Motivated by a charity function in Medellín, it was the author's avowed favorite. In this short novel, the grandiose La Blanca Falls and the Andean mountainside provide the majestic setting for what Federico de Onís describes as the dilemma of a girl torn between love and duty (*EPC*, II, xvii). In the delicacy of theme and treatment, *Hail, Regina* seems to continue the tradition of *Dimitas Arias* and, particularly, "Blanca," though the author scoffed at the latter as not being "up his alley," whereas Regina's story met with his unqualified approval.

Regina is delicate by temperament, submissive to authority. Her life is bedeviled by an overwhelming love for a man whose iniquities (which are never concretely defined) seem to disqualify him as her husband. Prayers are of no avail. Unable to banish the "terrible phantom of Marcial Rodríguez" from her heart, yet temperamentally incapable of defying the authority of parents and village priest, Regina's dilemma admits of no solution except death. Death comes to the saintly girl when the horrors of an epidemic lay waste to the village.

The focus in this short novel is entirely on Regina Duarte's dilemma. The object of her ill-fated affection, Marcial, is not drawn with Carrasquilla's customary care. He appears only once in the story, hurling defiance at his unknown maligners and challenging the truth of the village gossip. There is no further explanation, and Marcial vanishes as abruptly as he emerged, a colorless literary creation, truly more "phantom" than "terrible." Regina adores him; the villagers slander him; his black servant, Fraciquí, worships the very ground under his feet; and the author chooses to leave it at that. If Regina proves a fascinating, delicate creation, Marcial to me is one of the most perplexing and least satisfying ones.

This may have been designed so as not to divert attention from Regina's insoluble problem, which is intensified by her isolation in the village. Regina is truly a human being "out of rapport with her environment" (*EPC*, I, 180).

Two further characters in *Hail, Regina* merit a word of comment—namely Fraciquí and the priest. The former is one of those attractive colored servant figures to whose unconditional loyalty the author pays tribute on a number of occasions.[20] Fraciquí adores his young master, Marcial, because his wretched existence improved radically when he became part of the Rodríguez household.

The priest is a strange-looking figure of irresistible spiritual magic. Very different from Father Casafús, he communicates effectively with every one of his listeners, his most immediate vehicle being his tears. His popularity is unquestioned, and each of his visits in the village turns into a spontaneous triumph. Speaking the language of his parishioners, his approach pays spiritual dividends.

Notwithstanding the author's personal preference, *Hail, Regina* is clearly lacking in psychological insight and displays marked defects in the handling of the story. This "poem in prose," which contains some of the author's most exquisite lines of narrative,[21] is redeemed by its stylistic excellence.

To sum up the author's initial creative phase, Carrasquilla shows his narrative mettle and his consummate skill at reproducing authentic regional speech. He demonstrates that he enjoys telling his stories and that he tells them well. His first child characters point to the beginnings of a lifelong interest in young people.

As yet, his writings give few indications of psychological probing: there is only spasmodic evidence of concern with the complexities of the human heart. The characters which he depicts are often monolithic, black and white, heavily underlined. The living shade of grey is as yet absent. Finally, the regional setting is not yet integrated with the human interest and remains little more than a colorful backdrop.

There are two further symptoms of this period of literary apprenticeship—namely, the semblance of a plot and the odd example of didacticism, both of which he is to discard as his career progresses.

Three works stand out from this phase: *Dimitas Arias*, "Little Saint Anthony," and above all, "In the Right Hand of the Father." Showing Carrasquilla the master storyteller, they also point to the three essential themes of his creative work as a whole—namely, the folkloric, the child character, and the humble being consumed by a single idea.

CHAPTER 5

The Observer of Human Weakness (1906–1921)

A deceptively simple story opens the author's second period. "Simon Magus," we recall, was hurriedly scribbled for "the members only"; A Child's Heart evokes "futilities from days gone by" (EPC, I, 197). Published in 1906, it is one of the three most searching child studies from Carrasquilla's pen. After sixteen years of literary activity, the author's psychological vision is beginning to deepen, and from now on his stylistic mastery will be coupled with a more penetrating portrayal of the human heart. Fleeting glimpses, foreshadowing this broadening process in the author's creative genius, can be found in such delicate cuentos as "Blanca" and particularly in Dimitas Arias.

I   A Child's Heart

In A Child's Heart, Carrasquilla observes human growth during its formative years and discovers how from a confusion of conflicting impressions and sensations there gradually emerges the pattern of a personality. Autobiographical echoes are unmistakeable in this novel, as unmistakeable as is the interest of the author in the reactions of young people. Paco, the youthful hero of A Child's Heart, at first sight strikes us as a typical boy of the region raised in a deeply religious environment. But when we look at him more closely, we soon realize that, the same as Regina, the same as Blanca, the same as the boy in "Simon Magus," young Paco is out of tune with his environment as well as with his contemporaries. The boy is obsessed with what is beautiful. Beauty delights him, whereas the ugly brings out his most sadistic instincts. "Toads are my personal enemies" he candidly confesses (EPC, I, 201), and his nebulous search for beauty prompts him to reject his personal enemies so violently that he goes so far as tying their legs together and roasting them over a slow fire. When his father metes out punishment, the boy feels deeply humiliated and, accompanied by his faithful dog Mentor, runs away from home, determined never to return. His emotional crisis is resolved by very real pangs of hunger which prove stronger than his extravagant thoughts of vengeance.

Paco's bond with his mother and, above all, his "saintly grandmother" is strong; he seems to have little in common with his father, whom he tends to treat with condescension. As far as his brothers and the rest of his contemporaries are concerned, Paco's attitude is one of romantic contempt. Their interests are not his, and he makes no effort to hide his scorn for what he considers "pure scum" (*EPC*, I, 235).

The principal character who emerges from *A Child's Heart* is not humanly attractive. Paco is vain and arrogant and given to fits of temper. Hypersensitive, he bursts into tears at the slightest provocation. Under the deceptive disguise of "futilities from days gone by," Carrasquilla inquires into the complex character of a little boy who becomes increasingly concerned with beauty until it verges on an obsession. The barbarous roasting which Paco administers to the toads and the deliberate beating of the mules which his father interprets as wanton sadism and punishes accordingly must be seen within the context of his complete character pattern to be understood. The contempt which he professes toward his brothers and his generation as a whole for devoting time to such humdrum pursuits as agriculture is part of the same pattern. So is the revulsion which his teacher inspires in him. "Since I was not able to roast him like the toads or beat him like the mules, I killed him in effigy" ("ya que no me era posible tostarlo, como a los sapos, ni apalearlo como a las mulas, le mataba en efigie"—*EPC*, I, 236), the boy admits.

The spontaneous search for beauty, which he can never capture and which he cannot even define—whenever he feels that it is within his reach, it turns to smoke (*EPC*, I, 249)—causes him to seek guidance from his mother and his grandmother. These two characters, next to the hero himself, are drawn with the greatest care.

Paco's mother, the "countess," is depicted with genuine affection.

She is an admirable woman who will not tolerate slights against her family. Among the most revealing episodes is one when Paco's father pokes good-natured fun at his wife's family and Doña Beatriz picks up the gauntlet with dignity and eloquence. Paco, who has not missed a word of the verbal duel, takes a lasting impression away with him.

The grandmother, Elvira, is another deeply human figure, and a guiding star for young Paco. Her seventy-six years have not affected her physically or mentally. As far as the boy is concerned, her position is clearly central: she is "the sun of that system" (*EPC*, I, 226). When she dies at the end of the novel, Paco's reaction is one of shocked disbelief. He does not fly into a rage. One of his guiding lights has been snuffed out by God's inexorable will, and the child is temporarily stunned. He is not the same Paquito as before, remarks the author (*EPC*, I, 257).

Summing up, this "model of child psychology,"[1] which stands at the threshold of the second phase in Carrasquilla's prose fiction, clearly faces two ways. The hypersensitive child brings to mind the central episodes of both "Simon Magus" and "Blanca," while the maladjustment reminds us of Regina, who is equally out of sympathy with her environment. However, the obsessive search for "the beautiful" which lies at the root of the boy's sense of superiority and his delusions of grandeur contain in embryonic form the overwhelming desires which characterize, and frequently confound, the lives of Carrasquilla's adult characters.

II "*Myrrh*"

In 1907, the fragment of a story appeared in the periodical *Alpha* in Medellín. It was dedicated to Alfonso Castro "as public apology," a note which brings to mind the open letter episode and the flurry surrounding the publication of Castro's "Spiritual Daughter."

Four pages make up the fragmentary story, and one cannot help wondering why the "public apology" remained unfinished. Some twenty-five years later, the essay "Pax et concordia" was to serve a similar purpose—namely, reconciliation with Dr. Castro, which the fragmentary story "Myrrh" ("Mirra") apparently did not accomplish.

The story opens with a glimpse of a boudoir where Cruz and Elisa Albano are preparing for a "big event" by running over possible girl's and boy's names for the hundredth time. Soon the scene shifts to the husband's room, which though not observing the meticulous symmetry of Agustín's abode (in *Fruits of my Homeland*), fails to display what Carrasquilla terms the "deliberate disorder of nowadays" (*EPC*, I, 585). Indeed, it appears to be an appropriate blend of order and disorder from which the color red has been whimsically banished.

Cruz Albano is a musician, and throughout the story, musical allusions abound, with specific references to Wagner, Beethoven, Chopin, and Godard. After reciting some poetry to his wife, Cruz sits down at the piano. When he has finished playing, Elisa is hypnotized. The bewitching tune which she attributed to Beethoven turns out to be by a popular Venezuelan contemporary, Teresa Carreño, "almost Beethoven" (*EPC*, I, 587).[2] Here the glimpse fades out.

There are a number of interesting elements in this inconsequential story fragment. First of all, the human intimacy of the two young people who argue playfully about the sex and name of the prospective baby; second, the artistic atmosphere in the Albano household, due undoubtedly to the husband's interests (who seems to have "civilized" Elisa); and finally—a climax—the masterly description of the hypnotic power of music. The milieu is one of *modernista* refinement. The unfinished story has distinct possibilities: in setting it serves as a preamble to the work which appears three years later—*Grandeur*, a novel about Medellín's upper middle class.

The fragment "Myrrh" proves, if proof were needed, that Carrasquilla, while censuring certain extremes, does not reject the literary equipment of *modernismo* as such. The fragment is worthy of note chiefly because it shows that, less than a year after critically discussing in his two "Homilies" *modernista* technique as applied to the Antioqueño setting (see Chapter 3), Carrasquilla writes a short story in the *modernista* mode, the message of which is essentially aesthetic, with little thought content but a great deal of sensual effect.

III Grandeur

Grandeur, published in 1910 (and dedicated to "my friend Susana Olózaga de Cabo"), is the story of a mother whose daughters constitute her only purpose in life. According to Horacio Bejarano Díaz,

it is the least known among the author's four major novels. (Antonio
Curcio Altamar's study of the Colombian novel does not discuss it
at all.)

Carrasquilla's own introduction, as usual, is of the utmost simplicity. Having scribbled "Simon Magus," evoked "futilities from
days gone by" in *A Child's Heart,* he claims, in the novel *Grandeur,*
to "bring together . . . notes, characters, and details of our milieu."[3]
The setting is Medellín, the same as in *Fruits of my Homeland* and,
more recently, in the "Myrrh" fragment. Central among a picturesque array of human beings is Juana de Samudio, who has climbed
the social ladder tenaciously from humble beginnings, in order that
her daughters may marry well. She is haunted by a "neurosis of
grandeur" (*EPC,* I, 271), which she regards as an essential prerequisite for her daughters' marital happiness. She herself had been
married at fifteen and became a widow at twenty-three; she always
lived in the country, with mass her only major outing. Since her
arrival in Medellín, she has been perpetually on her guard, suspecting slights at every social encounter. Social recognition is her
main objective in life, not for her own sake, but for that of her
daughters' future.

Two events spell fleeting triumph and lasting economic ruin for
this vain and shallow woman who casts all caution to the winds
when her daughters are involved. Not only does she attend the
sumptuous costume ball, but, to belie persistent rumors about her
precarious economic situation, Doña Juana herself throws a gala
party which she finances by pawning her jewels. For a while, things
seem to be going well, and the mother basks in her daughter's
happiness. When the reaction sets in, Juana finds herself alone and
"without object in life" (*EPC,* I, 370). The bankruptcy of her son-
in-law, one of the melancholy aftereffects of the spectacular wedding, coupled with other ill-fated business transactions, paradoxi-
cally restores a purpose to her life. Her compulsive desire to "shine
again" in society uses her own daughters as tools, despite persistent
warnings from well-meaning friends. Doña Juana is determined to
do her duty, as she sees it, regardless of the consequences. Comments the author: "No one can be blamed for having an erroneous
or deformed conscience" ("Nadie tiene la culpa de tener conciencia
errónea o deformada"—*EPC,* I, 374). Doña Juana's misguided motherly love not only brings about the economic ruin of the family, but
also precipitates her son's death.

There may be a remote analogy between Juana de Samudio and Agustín Alzate, two victims of "grandeur neurosis." It is obvious, of course, that the former may claim extenuating circumstances which are not admissible in the case of the latter. Agustín is a totally "rotten fruit" with no redeeming features, whereas Juana de Samudio's ill-advised actions are prompted by a positive motherly instinct—the author describes her as a "self-denying mother" (*EPC*, I, 374)—which assumes obsessive proportions. She represents a rather common human phenomenon. In her desperate efforts to maintain a splendid exterior, at the cost of undermining the family economy, she will go to any length "to keep up with the Joneses." (Maintaining the shining façade while fire may be raging inside is a genuinely Hispanic trait which brings to mind the penniless nobleman in the picaresque classic *Lazarillo de Tormes* who prefers to endure hardship and privations rather than admit that he is destitute.)

Juana's two daughters, motivating powers of her life, have little in common. Tutú is a sugar doll (*EPC*, I, 263), vain and shallow, truly a chip off the old block. Magdalena, Magola for short, on the other hand, is a woman whose common sense enables her to pierce the environmental shell and to appraise people irrespective of their social or financial stamp. Essentially kind, she does not mince matters when the occasion demands it. One such occasion is that visit of Leonilde de Gama, whose malicious barbs cause Magola to defend her family with eloquent ingenuity and to resort to a verbal battery thinly covered by cultured veneer. She is no less eloquent but considerably more ironical in taking her brother to task for his brusque behavior toward their mother.

There are two episodes particularly which serve to throw Magola's personality into bold relief, and significantly enough, both episodes shock Doña Juana profoundly, because her daughter's human and humane conduct offends her warped sense of values. First, Magola causes elegant eyebrows to go up when, at a gala party, she invites an obscure bullfighter to her table, leaving by dint of a few kind words and a smile a warm glow in a life of failure and disillusionment. As a result of her attention, the poor wretch suspects for the first time in his life that he might be "a human being like anyone else" (*EPC*, I, 317). But there is a more telling incident to test Magola's character. While she is in the midst of a gay party, the news arrives that the corsetmaker's son has suffered a severe accident. Rushing to the scene of the disaster, Magola is overwhelmed by the stark contrast between the luxury of the elegant party and the squalor of the working class hovel. A friendly smile and a few kind words evidently do not suffice in this situation, and Magola spontaneously solicits financial aid for the destitute family by personally canvassing the elegant tables, to her mother's stunned disbelief.

Intelligent, kind, charitable, giving light by word and by deed, Magdalena Samudio is a delightful creation, doubtless one of the most attractive among all of Carrasquilla's novelesque characters; "enchanting" is the word which the novelist himself uses to describe her. The character of Magdalena is a fine tribute to Susana Olózaga de Cabo, the "distinguished Medellín lady" who honors him with her friendship, according to the "Few Words" of prologue to the novel.

Chichí, Magola's brother, is permanently at odds with his mother. He opposed their move to the city, considering the country a more appropriate setting for the family. All his critical comments on this subject strike Doña Juana as deliberate affronts, indeed, as attempts to keep the family in humble circumstances and to prevent their rise in the world. Between Doña Juana, who gauges this rise in terms of her daughters' advantageous marriages, and her brusque son there is no common ground. Beneath his uncouth exterior, Chichí has a strongly developed sense of self-respect, which he jealously defends. Chichí is blinded by his personal brand of "true nobility," a subject on which he never tires of lecturing his mother. Concluding one of his tirades with these significant words—"Your son is a gentleman . . . he understands true honor and true dignity"—he implies of course a monopoly position as far as these commodities are concerned. Chichí's unbending behavior pattern leads to his tragic end in a duel in defense of his sister's honor.

There are some interesting parallels and some marked differences between Chichí and his sister Magola. Both are refreshingly forthright and endowed with a sound dose of common sense, in contrast with the other two members of the Samudio household, who are blinded by appearances. But while Chichí carries his sincerity to a brusque extreme, unwittingly defeating his own purpose in his social and human relations, Magola's maturity knows when to temper candor with wisdom. She, by the way, is the only one in the family who is able to communicate effectively with rough Chichí, reaching out to that heart which is "so roguish in appearances, so good in essence" (*EPC*, I, 299).

The tenuous novelistic plot, habitual in Carrasquilla's writings, receives part of its impetus from Doña Leonilde de Gama, who bitterly resents the social triumphs of the Samudio *parvenus* (particularly because the charming Samudio girls prove a great deal more attractive than her own daughters). Jealousy and envy are the mainsprings of her actions, and she does her utmost to eliminate the rivals to her daughters' social success by means fair or foul, achieving, of course, the very opposite, by making Doña Juana increasingly determined to fight for her place in the "social sun," for the sake of her daughters.

Doña Leonilde's husband, Bernardo, placing common sense above family loyalty, shows his admiration for Magola by lending support to any cause which she champions. Ignoring his wife's furrowed brow, he responds to Magola's charity appeal by handing over his entire poker gains. Pleading for tolerance and for "live and let live," he upbraids Doña Leonilde for shallowness and hypocrisy in matters of religion, for being excessively concerned with the souls of others and paying too little attention to her own: "A lot of Christ on the outside" he exclaims in disgust, "and, inside, the devil" (*EPC*, I, 354).

Their son, Renato, is perhaps the most tragic figure in this novel. Raised in an atmosphere of plenty, he tries to give a purpose to his futile existence by discreetly aiding the Samudio family when Doña Juana's imprudent acts of "brinkmanship" have led to melancholy consequences. Tragically, it is Renato's generous intent which, coupled with Doña Juana's ill-fated and ill-timed endeavor to "shine again," sets Medellín's tongues wagging and precipitates the duel between Renato and Chichí in which the latter is killed.

Fourteen years separate *Fruits of my Homeland* from *Grandeur*. Very much the same setting pertains to both novels: Medellín and a human array of humble peasant origin. Some try to conceal the latter, only to make it more evident: they are the money aristocracy. As human beings, Juana or Leonilde may be less repulsive than Agustín and Filomena; socially there is very little difference between them.

Despite these similarities, *Grandeur* is the more mature work because it is less monolithic. Its psychological probing continues the trend of *A Child's Heart,* but encompasses a broader human spectrum. It has both greater individual complexity and greater social variety. It depicts wealth and misery, lofty ideals and plain common sense, hypocrisy and candor. It offers a human mosaic composed of the world of business, as well as intellectuals, artists, and men of letters. It holds the mirror to shallow society, contrasting it with the occasional glimpse of beautiful nature.

Overshadowing all is the mainspring of the action, a mother's love for her daughters. To use Mark Twain's words, Juana de Samudio is a good woman "in the worst sense of the word." Incapable of viewing the world around her in terms other than her daughters' future, she will run any risk to insure their happiness. It is that obsessive love which invites disaster, and gloom settles inexorably over the home of the woman whose maternal affection verges on madness.[4]

Grandeur was followed by a set of short stories. Some of these betray a "chronicle" *(crónica)* or "sketch of customs" *(cuadro)* flavor and attain "short story" *(cuento)* status because of living characters who testify to a new orientation in Carrasquilla's creative genius. In this second phase, his colorful narrative receives added human impetus through convincing character creations.

IV *"Etymological Tale"*

"Etymological Tale" ("Historia etimológica") is the story of Luz, a charming prostitute. Lending variety and enchantment to the routine life in Gabelagrande, she allows her light to shine equally on the poor and on the rich. Her life-giving qualities, which the author likens to those of the sun, are not appreciated by the women in the district, who charge that husbands are known to keep their families on bread and water, while squandering their money on champagne parties for Luz, and that irresponsible sons shower her with stolen family jewelry. A villagewide boycott of the girl results in a general reluctance to mention her name, which interestingly enough comes to be asssociated with the powers of darkness. Such is the stigma attached to the name "Luz" that villagers studiously avoid mentioning light of any description, even electrical.

The scandal reaches its peak when Don Rodrigo de la Guarda appears to be yielding to Luz's charms. Don Rodrigo is a perfect gentleman and an eligible bachelor of considerable means, indeed, the dream of the mothers of all marriageable daughters of good society in Gabelagrande. There is a pattern about Don Rodrigo's visits. He calls on Luz regularly once a week, every Sunday after mass, spends exactly one hour with her in complete privacy, and then takes his leave.

And what happens after the door has closed behind them and the two are alone? Seated at a safe distance—and here is the unexpected ending for the *cuento*—she receives instruction in reciting poetry. Neither he nor she ever reveals the true purpose of their weekly meetings, and the reader only finds out because the "hobgoblin author" allows him to peep through the keyhole.

But once, when her companions persist in questioning her about the personal qualities of Don Rodrigo, Luz answers with a slightly mischievous smile: "Don Rodrigo? . . . Oh, he is just appearances, nothing more" ("¡No es sino elegante!"—*EPC*, II, 607). The phrase soon becomes notorious and even spreads to Medellín, where it is used to the present day to describe a person whose bark is worse than his bite, who is all façade and little substance. This charming little story with its unexpected denouement brings to mind Ricardo Palma's *Peruvian Traditions (Tradiciones peruanas)*. Like many of the latter, it traces the origin of a popular saying, doing so with colorful detail and with a picaresque smile.

V *"The Preface of Francisco Vera"*

"The Preface of Francisco Vera" ("El prefacio de Francisco Vera"), published a fortnight later, is the story of a man who terrorizes an entire community in a variety of ways, while giving the most loyal support to the coffers of the church. The parish priest, detecting a glimmer of hope in Vera's generosity, exacts from him a vow to turn over a new leaf. Turn it over he does indeed, but the new leaf proves worse than the old one. Crowning his career of evildoing with supreme blasphemy, he forces sacrilege upon the village priest. The latter never recovers from the ordeal and, deeply disillusioned, pleads with his parishioners to bring the criminal to justice. Francisco Vera dies as a penitent sinner.

While reaching the conclusion that our Heavenly Lady not only "redeems the captives of infidels, but snatches from the devil the souls which he already has in his claws" ("no sólo redime los cautivos de infieles, sino que le arranca al Diablo las almas que ya tiene entre sus garras"—*EPC*, I, 592), Carrasquilla does not have the slightest intention of teaching a lesson in theology. "The Preface of Francisco Vera" is simply another one of those picturesque folk tales in the vein of "In the Right Hand of the Father" and "The Lonely Soul" in which the delight of telling a story takes precedence over character delineation. Firmly rooted in popular tradition, its subject matter, observes Onís, brings to mind the "priest's ballad referred to in *Don Quixote*."⁵ Any folk tale told by Carrasquilla acquires a peculiar charm of human directness. The reader therefore is quite ready to believe that it is not an "invented story" but rather an "example" which happened in every last detail "just as your servant learnt it" (*EPC*, I, 588).

VI *"The Great Prize"*

"The Great Prize" ("El gran premio") is another such "authentic" tale which emphasizes its folk flavor from the very introductory formula of "Once upon a time." It tells of a poor wretch who has a saintly wife, a numerous family, and nothing to eat. He seems to be one of those people "perpetually superfluous in life" (*EPC*, I, 598). A curious sense of self-respect makes him scorn manual labor (very much in the Hispanic tradition), and instead of working with his hands, he is constantly busy "doing nothing." When his frugal table is suddenly blessed with a magic meal, he slights the obvious supernatural guest because he feels that the latter has slighted him all his life. Instead, he invites death to be his dinner guest, because death bestows his gifts on rich and poor alike. Her "August Majesty," though impervious to Bacchus' delights ("I belong to the temperance lodge" she observes—*EPC*, I, 601) shows her appreciation with a "great prize." The poor man henceforth can ask for anything he likes and be sure of fulfilment, with the significant exception of salvation. Since then he has been stalking the world, pride and arrogance incarnate, in constant metamorphosis, the "terrible man" in every century of our era (*EPC*, I, 602).

This story has clear links with "In the Right Hand of the Father." Both stories endow supernatural characters with charmingly local flavor. While "The Great Prize" shows the deserts of pride and arrogance in human relations, Peralta's humility receives its well-earned reward for all eternity.

VII *Four Contemporary Stories*

The two tales involving the supernatural were followed by four contemporary stories, two in 1914 and two in 1915, which the author built around one of his favorite psychological themes. In "The Pearl" ("La perla"), first published under the title "Holy Week" ("Semana Santa"), "The Angel" (El angel"), "The Plant" ("La mata"), and "The Toy Gun" ("El rifle"), a melancholy piece of humanity achieves a glimpse of happiness by reaching out for a humble object which becomes more important than life itself. The cycle of four shows faint echoes of "Simon Magus" and more distinct ones of "Blanca" and *Dimitás Arias*.

Two angel statues in the Easter procession bring momentary fulfilment to a sad life of poverty and disillusionment, as Rosa María, nicknamed "The Pearl" because of her exemplary conduct, is on her deathbed in the last stages of a rapid fever. The story probes the mind and heart of the girl whose humble dreams center around the two angels which her hands and devotion have laboriously shaped. Its psychological searching testifies to the deepening of the human focus during the second phase in the author's career.

Stark poverty envelops Felicita and Fortunata ("The Angel"), who live in a "Persian splendor of misery" (*EPC*, I, 594), the mother bedridden for seven years with neuralgia, the daughter infirm, but compelled to go begging to eke out a meager existence. Branded as a witch by the villagers, Fortunata's daily path is a calvary. Some offer her charity to get rid of her, but most slam their doors in her face or curse her under their breath. If it had not been for the priest's aid, the two would have died long ago.

Things change with the visit by Mario Naos, a vacationing law student, whose curiosity is aroused by the ramshackle homestead on the outskirts of the village of Sambruno. On learning the old woman's tale of woe, Naos decides to play angel. He feeds them and departs with the promise that the Virgin (through his intercession) would look after them from now on. Naos does not forget his promise, and Felicita and Fortunata are given lodging. "They never saw the angel again," concludes Carrasquilla "because God's spirits come to earth only once" ("no han vuelto a ver al angel, porque los espíritus de Dios sólo una vez bajan a la tierra"—*EPC*, I, 597).

While "The Pearl" is purely narrative, "The Angel" adds colorful dialogue to the romantic intervention of a wealthy law student who brings "angelic" powers to bear where the villagers fail. In telling this story, Carrasquilla once more denounces ignorance and prejudice on the part of all those "good people" who are repelled by externals and who refuse to come to grips with essential human values. Fortunata's filial love, which keeps her mother alive, is completely overshadowed, in the eyes of the worthy citizens of Sambruno, by the hump which deforms her back. "Charity toward the repulsive neighbor does not dwell in all hearts," is the author's caustic comment (*EPC*, I, 595). "The Angel" remains a good story even without the moral twist.

In "The Plant," María Engracia encounters an "angel" who assumes the form of a plant, lighting up her squalid existence. The story of María Engracia is a depressingly common one. She comes to the city as a young girl, only to lose her virtue at the hands of an unscrupulous seducer who takes advantage of her lack of worldly wisdom to ravage her beauty. Abandoned by everyone, María Engracia lives in misery and complete isolation, constantly threatened with eviction by an unfeeling landlord.

One day she happens to come across a shoot which has dropped off a moving van. Planting it in a pot, she places it near the entrance of her bare abode. Soon the shoot begins to grow into a fine plant, attracting the attention of passers-by and eventually turning into a bridge between María Engracia and life. The plant becomes María Engracia's major preoccupation because it restores to her that living contact with the world around her of which callous behavior has deprived her. She begins to take an interest in her milieu again, then in her own person; finally, her faith is restored. In short, by virtue of that shoot which grows into a plant, "that spirit which seemed to be dead revived" (*EPC*, I, 614). The plant becomes so central to her universe that, when the brutal landlord destroys it, María Engracia collapses. In her final delirium, she has the glorious vision of her very own plant ushering her into paradise "like the arch of triumph" (*EPC*, I, 614)—the symbol of divine compassion redeeming a squalid existence.

The story of María Engracia doubtless is a more fascinating human phenomenon than that which prompts Naos to assume angelic functions during one of his outings ("The Angel"). While the tribulations of Felicita and Fortunata are depicted largely in their material ramifications, María Engracia's hunger proves more spiritual than physical.

To me, "The Plant" is a remarkable story also because of its succinctness. Carrasquilla succeeds in capturing a moving human experience in the briefest possible space, without any dialogue.[6]

A short while later, "The Toy Gun" appeared. The setting is Bogotá, a rare occurrence in Carrasquilla's writings, which on the whole are tied to Antioquia as inseparably as is his life. In the midst of the gay Christmas Eve crowd, busily engaged in selecting gifts, two people meet, and this meeting gives momentary happiness to both of them. On one side there is a gentleman of melancholy mien, childless, separated from his wife, and a stranger in the capital, more keenly conscious of his loneliness while seeing himself surrounded by happy-looking people. On the other, a street urchin, offering him a shoeshine. When a toy gun accidentally drops out of a package of a passer-by, the boy's face reveals such unmitigated delight that his customer decides to buy him one as a reward for his services. The toy gun, which in the life of the donor fills a vital need—namely, that of bestowing gifts at Christmas time, on that day when "tribute is paid to the family" (*EPC*, I, 607)—constitutes the first warm glow in the boy's wretched life since his mother died. For the little shoeshine boy, the gun is a great deal more than a handsome toy; it stands for that one moment of happiness, when someone treats him like a human being. The gift, then, not only lights up the donor's lonely mood but has a message of hope for the eleven year old recipient. When his stepmother, whose interest in the boy does not go beyond the earnings which he delivers to her every evening, smashes the gun in a fit of temper, life loses its meaning for him. The heartless stepmother, the same as the brutal landlord in "The Plant," shatters a human life through callous, unfeeling action. "Take me away, mother" is Tista's final pleading as the curtain goes down over the moving tale of a Bogotá shoeshine boy whose melancholy life finds temporary fulfillment in a "toy gun."[7]

VIII *The Seven "Aquarels"*

In 1919 and 1920, Carrasquilla composed seven pieces which he termed "Aquarels" ("Acuarelas"). By that time, the novelist was back from his second trip to the capital. The "Aquarels" are brief scenes which portray some simple aspect of life in Antioquia or which paint a mood—thumbnail sketches, as it were, which have sufficient human interest to endow them with short story flavor.

Vitality is the dominant mood pervading Aquarel A, entitled "The Child of Happiness" ("El hijo de la dicha"). Tuco, from unknown parentage, is regarded as the son of the mining community. He is a happy little fellow, reflecting the successful experiment in socialization under which the community as a whole feels responsible for his well-being. Rolling around in the dung heap and bubbling over with vitality, he is indeed the symbol of health, happiness, and life. A note of momentary anxiety enters when one day happy Tuco becomes unwittingly embroiled in a fight between a brooding hen and two turkey buzzards in which feathers, dung, and earth fly copiously. The hen puts her enemies to flight, but poor little Tuco comes close to losing his life, lying on the ground pale and lifeless, reenacting the "role of Belgium" between the formidable powers.

Vitality triumphs over temporary reverses in "The Child of Happiness" (since Tuco is eventually revived). "Palonegro" (Aquarel B), on the other hand, reflects unmitigated gloom. It is imbued from the outset with a mood of foreboding and melancholy suspense, relating to the fate of the young man who left the house at daybreak with his dog Palonegro never to return. More and more details come to be filled into the sketch as the story develops, until the reader is as convinced as the old woman Custodia in the first paragraph that some mishap must have occurred. The young man has "either drowned in the river or has been bitten by a snake" ("o ahogado en el río, o picado de culebra"—*EPC*, I, 643). The truth is far more tragic, and the final glimpse is that of the body of the suicide; of the mourning grandmother and child; and of the despondent dog, Palonegro, with a heart "more loving and gentle than that of a child" ("más amoroso y tierno que el corazón de un niño"— *EPC*, I, 645), whose overwhelming sorrow reverberates in the night.

Aquarels C and D, published in reverse chronological order in Medellín's *El Espectador*, share a common theme, centering around the yearning for momentary recognition in an obscure life. Aquarel D, entitled "The Cyrenians" ("Los cirineos"), depicts two humble carpenters, Rufo and Rufito, father and son, who climax their regular devotional activities by participating in the Good Friday procession. Fanatic loyalty to the holy cross—product of his own hands—and to the Cyrenian's role are the keys to the father's obscure existence. There is something deeply lovable about this "carpenter of the cross" who dedicates his whole life to the one purpose and who raises his son in the same spirit, oblivious to the snickering of the villagers, who regard both of them as crazy.

The humble lives of Rufo and Rufito have their one brilliant moment every year during Holy Week. The lives of Doña Felicinda Peraza and her four daughters in Aquarel C, "Brilliance for a Moment" ("Fulgor de un instante"), are totally devoid of brilliance. Not even the village gossip recognizes their existence. They are simply ignored, until one day the incredible happens and the guest list of a gala reception includes the names of the Perazas.

The mother's excitement on receiving the official invitation might be compared to that of the mother in *Grandeur* under similar circumstances. The same as Doña Juana, Doña Felicinda hesitates for some time, wondering whether or not to accept the invitation. She finally does accept, conscious of her "social duty." Alas, despite the most elaborate rehearsals and elegant clothes, the imagined social triumph turns into dismal failure, because in the course of the evening's entertainment, mother Felicinda inopportunely treats the village élite to an embarrassing "number which was not on the program" (*EPC*, I, 648). Goaded by alcohol and by the size of her audience, she confesses the whole precarious history of her family's participation in this elegant affair. The brilliance proves hollow indeed. The Perazas, "idols of a day" (*EPC*, I, 649), who, like Doña Juana (in *Grandeur*), bought their notoriety at the cost of substantial material sacrifice, drop back into obscurity with an audible bang after being subjected to public ridicule. "Brilliance for a Moment" may well illustrate the proverb "Even though the monkey may dress in silk, he still remains a monkey" ("Aunque el mono se vista de seda, mono se queda"). Carrasquilla has no use for hollow social brilliance and pretentiousness of any description. Felicinda's embarrassing conduct shows up the futility of straining for social recognition.

Aquarel E, entitled "Old Age Delights" ("Regodeos seniles"), depicts another lovable old factotum who has loyally served for generations. Sinforosa belongs to the family, and the children look up to her as they would to their own grandmother. She has now reached retirement, but as so often happens, finds it unthinkable to retire, interfering constantly around the house, while reflecting on the good old days and the wretched present (*EPC*, I, 653). Symbol of the former according to her is the genuine solid chocolate which everyone enjoys; symptom of the latter, that insipid liquid, based on a high water content, which she ingenuously terms "agualate" (*EPC*, I, 654).

Sinforosa has one major weakness: she loves eating and raids the larder continually. It seems impossible to break her of that bad habit, which harms the aging pilferer a great deal more than the provisions, which can easily be replenished. As a last resort, a crude but effective ruse is brought into play which cures the simple old woman forever. True, it almost kills her in the process, when her vivid imagination convinces her that her organism is being ravaged by the rat poison which one of the aunts claims to have added to the cheese.

Sinforosa is a vibrantly human creation, a servant figure reminiscent of Frutos ("Simon Magus") and anticipating Cantalicia in *Long Ago*. Her living, unspoiled personality, her human sentiments, and her authentic speech testify to the author's affectionate interest in that kind of a person and in her social class. (There can be little doubt that while Carrasquilla laughs *at* the Felicindas and the Doña Juanas, he laughs most heartily *with* the Sinforosas, the Frutos, and the Cantalicias.)

The story entitled "Superman" occurs almost in its entirety (except for the ending) in the second part of the trilogy *Long Ago*. Described in *EPC* as Aquarel F, "Superman" is more than twice the length of any of the other aquarels, which permits more careful character development.

The setting is La Blanca (reminiscent of *Hail, Regina*), a village nurtured for many years exclusively "by the miraculous milk of Christian doctrine" (*EPC*, I, 656) provided by the parish priest. One day, the government (the same as in *Dimitas Arias*) decides to open schools in the district, and Ceferino Guadalete appears on the scene. Appointed for the purpose of arousing La Blanca from its "slumber of ignorance" (*EPC*, I, 656), Don Ceferino proceeds at once to extend his influence into the ecclesiastical and civil spheres. He is a man of irresistible oratory, but totally lacking in intellectual and moral substance. He is one of those hollow shells with a glittering surface which Carrasquilla despises because they clamor for a brilliance which their human essence does not warrant.

Guadalete's despotic rule over La Blanca is based on blind acceptance of his intellectual superiority. When the latter is publicly called into question, Don Ceferino's empire crumbles. One of the senior grade pupils proves his undoing. Irene Carba not only protests against the corporal punishment which Guadalete administers lavishly, but challenges his authority by showing him to the villagers in his true "grandeur." The scandal which Irene's maverick rebellion precipitates leads to the tyrant's removal.

There are echoes of *Dimitas Arias* in the protagonist's professional status and to some extent in the rebellious girl pupil. However, whereas in *Dimitas Arias* the rebel does no more than make school life unbearable for a poor cripple, Irene resolutely unmasks an impostor. Ceferino Guadalete's essential hollowness, the same as that of Agustín Alzate, becomes evident as soon as someone stands up to him. Irene's fearless denunciation spells the end of a bully, just as Bengala's well-aimed blows precipitate the downfall of "King Augustus."

Guadalete's educational reforms doubtless bring benefits to the villagers of La Blanca, but they pay an exorbitant price in terms of personal freedom. The ultimate defeat of Don Ceferino, the "crushing of the serpent's head" (*EPC*, I, 663), therefore means liberation from the despotic rule of a fraud. Carrasquilla despises frauds no less than he detests despotism. The ignominious fall of the "superman" provides an illustration.

Aquarel G, "Philosophic Tranquility" ("Tranquilidad filosófica"), is the idyllic story of Liborio, Polonia, and the parrot Severiana, pride and joy of two "solitary adults." Liborio and Polonia have been married eleven years, and he might well be her son, such is the difference in their ages. Polonia is a prodigious worker; her hands never stand still. The regional delicacies which she prepares are offered partly for sale to the peons, but more particularly are intended to delight her husband's palate. In fact, her whole existence seems to hinge on three central pursuits; cater to Liborio, romp about with mischievous Severiana, and pray the rosary. Of course, her husband clearly stands first, and Carrasquilla takes pains to emphasize this preeminence by using the capital E whenever "El" ("He") refers to Liborio.

The rustic idyl, with never a ripple of trouble, finally prompts someone to ask a mischievous question, and Liborio volunteers an interesting reason for his blissful serenity. He is well looked after and enjoys life free from the disturbing symptoms of love. Since his wife is past her prime and not blessed with physical gifts, he is spared the pangs of jealously. "If I loved her I could not be so

constantly happy" ("Si fuera con amor no me mantenería tan con-
tento"—*EPC*, I, 667) is Liborio's unruffled retort as he returns to
his work.

In sum: the seven "Aquarels" which blend glimpses of character
creation with mood painting show a variety of human experience.
Focusing in turn on unbridled vitality, gloom and foreboding, touch-
ing devotion, ephemeral social triumph, precarious old age delights,
and hollow intellectual brilliance, they end on a note of "philosophic
tranquility," the result of Liborio's common sense approach to human affairs.

IX   Ligia Cruz

Ligia Cruz appeared in four numbers of *El Espectador* in November and December of 1920. In this short novel, the author
comes to grips with an obsession which reaches the proportions of
a mental derangement. The heroine has built for herself a world of
her own, based on her romantic readings. Not unlike Flaubert's
Emma Bovary, "she had always lived in a pure novel realm" (*EPC*,
I, 419), thoroughly out of touch, and out of tune, with her primitive
rural environment. The hazy urge to experience cosmopolitan plea-
sures in some distant city becomes accidentally identified with the
photograph of Mario Jácome, the son of her father's employer.
Falling in love with the picture, she proceeds to interpret a series
of chance happenings as part of an overall scheme designed by fate
to bring fulfillment to her dreams. Even her move to Medellín, for
reasons of health and education, is interpreted by the supersensitive
girl as an obvious intervention of providence to ensure her union
with Mario (whom, of course, she has never met).

It is at this point that the novel opens. On her arrival in Medellín,
the girl's heated imagination undergoes a severe test—the first of
many to follow—since the lady of the house is not at all happy about
the young visitor from the country and does not make the slightest
effort to hide her displeasure. So the welcome which the girl receives is anything but cordial, and the constant pinpricks aimed at
her inferior social status and at her unattractive exterior turn the
initial period of her stay into agony. Her situation improves only
when her godfather intervenes and recommends gently but firmly
that his family members practice true aristocracy in their everyday
behavior and start by being kind to their visitor. Once this first

hurdle has been overcome, the girl becomes increasingly confident. Her outer appearance, by dint of cosmetics and tailoring skill, soon undergoes a perplexing metamorphosis which she decides to accompany with a change of name. Dropping her name Petrona, she selects Ligia instead, in tribute to her favorite novel, *Quo Vadis*.

When Mario appears on the scene, Ligia is radiant, as her romantic dream seems to be on the verge of fulfillment. She does not realize that she is tottering on the brink of a nervous breakdown. Mario, who cannot help suspecting her mental instability from their first meeting, decides to utilize the intriguing combination of emotion and imagination for a scientific study. Ironically, whatever Mario does to probe her mental and emotional state intensifies her love for him, as she imagines herself requited by the young doctor.

When it becomes obvious to the latter that the girl's radiant exterior conceals a case of advanced tuberculosis, the scientist in Mario yields to the human being, who plays his part loyally to keep Ligia's great illusion alive until the end. Persuading her to agree to a change in climate, he promises to join her soon. Ligia tenaciously clings to his promise, which lights up her last moments on her lonely sickbed (just as the vision of her gorgeous plant redeems María Engracia's squalid existence). Spared that final horrible awakening, Ligia dies w ng for her beloved Mario and the car which will take them to l

Ligia's romantic obsessi s portrayed against a divided setting, some aspects of which th thor depicts directly, while he evokes others by means of flashback. On one hand there is the mining region, on the other, the "big city," Medellín. The human link is Silvestre Jácome, a resident of Medellín, but of mining stock and intimately connected wit he mining community. Jácome (whose name recalls the hero of t novel *Tierra virgen* [*Virgin Soil*] discussed in the critical ess "Heresies") evidently is the type of person of whom our auth proves. Devoid of artifice or synthetic polish, he is just a plain, it man with a good heart and plenty of common sense.

Ligia Cruz is a profoun book which probes deeply into character (even more deeply than *A Child's Heart*). Carrasquilla sets himself a tricky task and acquits himself well. The book is complex, the same as the emotions which smoulder, ready to be set ablaze at any moment. Indeed, one might say with Lubbock that "consciousness, no longer a matter of hearsay . . . is now before us in its original agitation."[8] Petrona Cruz is among Carrasquilla's most fascinating creations, and Mario's change from cold scientific enquiry to warm human concern shows the author's growing psychological insight.

Finally an interesting analogy comes to mind. In her failure to adjust to her milieu, her insistence on superimposing her own brand of reality, and her tenacious clinging to an illusion, Petrona Cruz is reminiscent of Emma Bovary. Carrasquilla's heroine, like that of Flaubert, is a Don Quixote "in skirts."

Curiously enough, the first publication of the novel, in *El Espectador*, attached to it the label "Aquarel H." There is in my view no common ground between the fleeting glimpses of human beings or moods necessarily rapid and superficial, which characterize the set of aquarels, and one of the most complex of Carrasquilla's character creations.

X *"What a Ball"*

"Happiness" is the theme of the short epilogue which Carrasquilla appended to this "melancholy irony of reality" (*EPC*, I, 629), written in 1921 and entitled "What a Ball!" ("Esta sí es bola"). The beginning of the story evokes "The Pearl" as well as "Blanca," in both of which an amateur artist looks approvingly at her own handiwork executed with assiduity and enthusiasm. Here, of course, the similarity ends. Rosa María's masterpiece is meant to embellish Holy Week celebrations in her native village, while Blanca pays her very personal tribute to the Virgin Mary: Blanca is concerned with the welfare of her family, Rosa María, with public worship. Julita Castañeda worships exclusively her own well-being, which she hopes to fashion mysteriously by dint of a perfectly shaped ball of silver paper.

Julita and her brother Millo busily drain their widowed mother's resources, she by her craze for fashion (which earns her the nickname "vitrine"), he by his ill-advised habit of carousing. The Castañeda trio, mother and the two children, are the perfect example of the newly rich, the country family transplanted into the city where their development is accompanied by severe growing pains. So-called "friends" do their best to intensify the latter. A momentary economic boom has imprudent repercussions in the Castañeda family. Millo squanders monstrous sums with unscrupulous companions. Julita finds the latest fashions irresistible to the point of folly, and Doña Ilduara yearns to travel to social acceptance on the keys of a pianola.

Like Juana Samudio, Ilduara Castañeda soon finds the price of notoriety exorbitant. There comes the inevitable rude awakening when their spending reaches alarming proportions, and her brother Eladio recommends an immediate return to the country. Doña Ilduara, unable to conceive of a life without a "social column," ignores the suggestion.

Her daughter meanwhile has become romantically involved with Javier Vallecilla, an engineering student whose chief assets consist in the maternal legacy which he hopes to receive the following year. Javier initiates the girl in the fascinating ritual of the "ball of happiness," the latest fad in a bankrupt economy where people cling to the ephemeral glitter of just about anything. Julia and Javier start their own *bola* with all the pomp and circumstance which the ritual prescribes, and from that solemn moment on, Julia can be seen working on her "happiness" at all hours. The reader's first glimpse of Julia is precisely during her favorite pastime, expertly tapping her own happiness and that of Javier (presumably in that order) into place. "Her folly and ignorance," observes the author, "are truly delightful" (*EPC*, I, 615). (A few years later and thousands of miles away, in Argentina, a related "magic" ritual embodies the hopes of another girl to whom an author attributes a folly and ignorance which are downright "delightful.")[9]

As the economic situation deteriorates and the mother stubbornly rejects a return to the country, the family goes downhill rapidly. Virtually all their belongings are in the pawn shop, and only the proceeds from the regular food-peddling expeditions by a loyal servant keep them alive. Millo sits at home, dejected, blaming universal injustice for depriving him of his vagabondries. Resembling an encaged porcupine, grunting occasionally to lament his lost paradise (*EPC*, I, 620), he is indeed a caricature of fallen grandeur, not unlike Agustín Alzate after Bengala's blows have stripped him of his grandiose shell.

While Ilduara has learnt to swallow her tears, Julia remains calm, convinced that her magic *bola* cannot possibly lie. Indulging in one of his caustic aphorisms, witty because of their very incongruity, Carrasquilla observes that since extremes touch, Julia would appear to share Saint Theresa's philosophy, dismissing all present tribulations as trifles "in view of the happiness which the future held in store for her" ("ante las dichas que la esperan, toda mortificación actual le es pasatiempo"—*EPC*, I, 620).

Yet Julia's trials have not yet begun. After a violent scene with her brother, who vainly tries to borrow money from her, the latter in a fit of rage snatches her beloved *bola* from her. When her good luck charm has disappeared, Julia is despondent. How is she to explain the loss to Javier? Doña Ilduara suggests that a new *bola* be substituted. The girl reluctantly agrees, but deep down she knows that the *Ersatz* cannot have the same magic powers and that her luck has run out. And so it seems at the end, with Millo in jail, the wedding postponed indefinitely, and mother and daughter on their way home—at last.

"What a Ball!" is an entertaining satire of a romantic fad. The heated imagination which identifies the magic paper ball with providence has traces of Petrona Cruz's lyrical extremes. The present story, however, does not attempt any psychological probing. The characters are types by and large, lacking in depth. Only loyal old Ubalda, radiating common sense, stands solidly on her feet. The emphasis is on the entertaining, though depressing, details of the episode (which Carrasquilla dedicates to two cousins, Lilí and Magda Moreno, the latter a talented novelist in her own right)[10] and on the moral lesson that happiness is just "a ball of shining paper

. . . which slips from our hands . . . and hurtles down . . . the slope of life ("una bola de papel radiante . . . que se escapa de las manos . . . y se despeña . . . por la . . . pendiente de la vida"—*EPC*, I, 629).

On this satirical note, the second phase in Carrasquilla's career, in which the author's human vision broadened and his psychological probing deepened and in which he matured noticeably, reached its conclusion. It was a period of the greatest variety in inspiration, reflected not only in his major works, but also in chronicles and sketches of customs (see Chapter 7), practically all of which originated during the decade between 1910 and 1920. It was also the period of the most persistent satire of shallowness and vanity. The ridiculous presumptuousness of Juana Samudio, Ernesta Jácome, and Ilduara Castañeda were given short shrift by Bernardo, Silvestre, and the loyal factotum Ubalda, demonstrating the author's common sense approach.

In terms of numbers, it was by far Carrasquilla's most productive phase, accounting for a total of well over eighty titles in a variety of genres. It proved a training ground for the final period, when complete integration of narrative, character, and milieu was achieved.

CHAPTER 6

The Spokesman of a Region (1922–1936)

CARRASQUILLA'S third period was most closely linked to his native milieu. There was no Bogotá trip to interrupt it. In striking contrast with the wealth of titles which marked the preceding phase, only four works originated during the final years. Any short pieces, such as chronicles, sketches of customs, or short stories, contemporary or supernatural in character, which may have been in the author's mind, did not reach literary autonomy, but were incorporated into the longer works. The latter spell out Carrasquilla's most mature creative achievement.

I The Blue-eyed Boy

The final period began in 1922 with the novel which has been described as "perhaps Carrasquilla's most intense and laboriously shaped work."[1] This work, *The Blue-eyed Boy*, seems to have much in common with *A Child's Heart*, which stands at the beginning of the second period. Both offer personal childhood recollections intermingled freely with fictional elements. Both follow the shaping of a boy's character through his formative years. Both record a number of conflicting impressions and sensations which gladden or sadden a boy's sensitive heart and which affect his development. The setting in both is a rural Antioqueño community.

Yet *The Blue-eyed Boy* is a far more complex work, chiefly because the impressions which assail the youth are more varied. There also exists a basic difference between the status of the two boys in the home and in the community. Paco, despite his extreme sensitivity and neurotic tendencies, is a native part of his milieu. Little Juan de la Rosa, on the other hand, is the son of unknown parents and

probably born out of wedlock. It soon becomes evident that the
little foundling hails from a social setting which is quite distant from
his foster parents' milieu.

The boy's position proves a precarious one from the beginning.
The villagers on the whole adore him. The aura of mystery which
surrounds him seems to enhance his appeal, but in his own foster
home he encounters much the same atmosphere of ill will which
poisoned Petrona Cruz' arrival in Medellín. However, while the
latter is made to suffer mainly psychological pin pricks—which hurt
no less deeply—the hostility which greets the little boy eventually
turns into blind hatred after his foster parent chooses to make Juan
de la Rosa his chief beneficiary. When hatred leads to physical
violence, Rumalda reacts with firmness and dignity and, in a memorable scene, (*EPC*, I, 504–505), she settles accounts with her entire
family for sins, past and present, which she has tended to overlook
until then. She reaches the agonizing conclusion that her nine children are her enemies whose base conduct is largely responsible for
her husband's mental derangement and his subsequent suicide.
Unable to vouch for the boy's safety in the village, she reluctantly
accepts the priest's offer to send him to Medellín to continue his
education. After making this painful decision, staunch Rumalda, a
tower of strength in adversity and a vigorous champion of her foster
child's rights, crumbles, sensing intuitively a vacuum in her life
which can never be filled.

Rumalda is a powerfully drawn figure of solid peasant stock with
a liberal dose of shrewdness and sound common sense, doubtless
one of the great character creations of the author. Her husband,
Higinio, is a more complex character. His suicide raises a variety
of questions. Can it really be blamed on the insidious behavior of
certain family members as Rumalda suggests in her final thundering
indictment, or is it primarily the result of Higinio's mental consti-
tution? There can be little doubt that the unsavory actions on the
part of others are at best a contributing factor, for the principal
motivating force is Higinio's pathological sense of guilt. The tough
peasant, scrupulously honest and fervently religious, goes down
under the relentless impact of his own conscience. Insanity precipitates suicide.

The "boy with the blue eyes" grows up between shrewd common
sense and mental instability, affectionately watched over by the
village priest. His mysterious appearance "out of nowhere" coin-

cides with the lowest ebb in the fortunes of Rumalda and Higinio, after the latter has lost his mining job. At the age of eleven, the boy stands out among his playmates. Outwardly he is as ragged as they, but his face and, above all, his delicate graceful hands clearly set him apart from the rest of the ragamuffins.

A host of new impressions crowd in upon the boy during a memorable Sunday visit to Medellín. Ancient churches arouse in him conflicting sensations as he is faced with century-old tradition under a decaying façade. The notions of crime and punishment enter his conscience when he meets a group of convicts under guard; a visit to the theater leaves him with the desire to be an orator.

On returning from the city, he finds it virtually impossible to adjust to the humdrum existence in the village. The Medellín trip has been a "sudden awakening" (*EPC*, I, 472), and the village routine threatens to asphyxiate him. He clashes continually with his former playmates, and the same as Paco, Regina, and Ligia Cruz, he ends up by isolating himself completely, driven by a sense of intellectual superiority.

The boy receives temporary psychological relief as well as moral and intellectual stimulation when the patron saint celebration is marked by a dramatic production and he is assigned a role in the play. Juan de la Rosa experiences his first emotional upset when he falls in love with the charming producer of the play and is in danger of being expelled from the cast because he cannot conceal his emotions. This delightfully human episode has no counterpart in any of the author's preceding child studies and brings to mind the psychological theme of an exquisite short novel by the Chilean Eduardo Barrios[2] which appeared a few years before Carrasquilla's novel. Barrios' child hero reacts violently when he sees his "beloved" kissed by her boyfriend. Juan de la Rosa, on the other hand, when seeing the object of his affection sitting in a box in her fiancé's company, extends a greeting with a rose in a gesture of "resigned gallantry" (*EPC*, I, 490).

The Blue-eyed Boy provides many such human touches. As usual, the details of the thin plot are secondary. What stands out are the three major characters and, more pronounced here than in any of the works of the preceding two periods, the unusual descriptive wealth of the picturesque region around them. Like Balzac, Carrasquilla cannot divorce his people from their organic setting. The latter's popular flavor emerges most typically in authentic popular speech (which does not preclude standard usage in narrative passages), regional food habits, and popular traditions, as well as folk songs and dances. Altogether, this all-pervading regional flavor—accentuated in *The Blue-eyed Boy* by the hero's peculiar status—adds a new dimension to the works of this final period in the author's career.

II *"Rogelio"*

Four years later, in 1926, Carrasquilla was to return to a favorite theme of his—namely, mysticism. "Rogelio" is the story of an eleven year old boy (the same age as Juan de la Rosa) who suffers from anemia, physically and spiritually. Raised in a totally irreligious milieu, he has never seen the inside of a church. This sickly little boy, whose dark melancholy eyes tell a sad tale, comes face to face with the Christ statue during the Holy Week procession. He is just one of the crowd watching the colorful proceedings when a sudden experience shakes him to his very depths. Christ moved his eyes to look at him! The boy's reaction is immediate; he cannot help following Christ, completely oblivious to the externals of the ritual. He is deaf to the music, blind to the spectacular apostles. He clings to Jesus with every fiber of his being, ever since He singles him out among the crowd.

Irresistibly attracted, he slips unnoticed into the sacristy where the figure is lodged. "Praying with his eyes shut, he sees Him better with the eyes of his soul" ("le reza con los ojos cerrados, y viéndolo mejor con los ojos del alma"—*EPC*, I, 636). The spiritual revelation (deepened by a prolonged exposure when he is inadvertently locked into the sacristy) affects him so lastingly that he enters the priesthood, restores his father to his rightful family, and leads his wretched mother to God.

In dedicating the story to his friend, the well-known short story writer Francisco Gómez (who wrote under the pseudonym of "Efe" Gómez), Carrasquilla describes it simply as "rugged in appearance, mystical in essence" (*EPC*, I, 630). No doubt Rogelio's spiritual ministry has clear points of contact with that of "Blanca." At this moment in his career, however, Carrasquilla evidently feels better prepared to handle a subject which in delicacy surpasses that of "Blanca." As far as I know, there is nothing in his correspondence to suggest any reluctance on his part to write the story. "Rogelio"

merits a significant place among Carrasquilla's writings not only
because of its literary qualities, psychological insight, and keen
observation,[3] but particularly because of the sympathetic, indeed
delicate, manner in which the author (sometimes accused of indif-
ference in spiritual matters) captures this most personal of all religious experiences. The account of Rogelio's spiritual awakening
is a fine example of Carrasquilla's sensitivity and good taste.[4]

III   The Marchioness of Yolombó

The Marchioness of Yolombó, Carrasquilla's greatest work according to Rafael Maya[5] and Curcio Altamar, seems to have matured
over a period of more than half a century before the author com-
mitted it to paper. Completed on January 19, 1926, the date which
appears on the last page of the manuscript, it was not published
until 1928.[6] Carrasquilla first became interested in Yolombó and its
picturesque colonial rule—so he tells us himself in a letter—through
his association with his great-grandfather, who was ninety-seven
when Carrasquilla was about eleven. The colorful details of the area
and the period which the old man evoked intrigued the boy: "I
lived glued to him like a little dog," the novelist confesses (*EPC,*
II, 811). The immediate stimulus, however, for composing the novel
stemmed from his grandfather Naranjo, who insisted that he "write
something about Yolombó and its marchioness." Thirty years were
to pass after the grandfather's death before Carrasquilla overcame
what he termed his "innate indolence" (*EPC,* II, 812).[7]

Prefacing *The Marchioness of Yolombó* is an elaborate prologue,
the only one of its kind among Carrasquilla's works. The latter is
designed to provide the reader with some facts and figures which
the author considers essential for an understanding of the regional
background and the historical period. He dismisses as hazardous
any attempt to reconstruct historical Yolombó on the basis of pres-
ent-day conditions, referring to the startling metamorphoses which
turned a semideserted area into an important colonial center during
the eighteenth century and which caused it to fade into insignifi-
cance in modern days.

Focusing upon the colonial era, Carrasquilla adorns a pseudo-
learned dissertation on the spirit of the age with such satirical
asides—true "Carrasquillisms"—as "the Spaniards never were
gentle shepherds for their American flock" ("los españoles nunca

fueron mansos pastores con el rebaño de estas sus Américas"—*EPC*, II, 18). Bonds of family and friendship would erode under the impact of greed. As far as members of the clergy are concerned, Carrasquilla is not impressed with their moral stature either, finding them excessively absorbed in temporal concerns rather than religious ones and all too ready to condone the abuses of the powerful.

In the absence of archives and official documents, Carrasquilla cites "oral tradition" as his only source, things he has heard from "old men and women." Consequently, what follows in novel form is no more than a "conjecture concerning that period and its people" (*EPC*, II, 21). So much for the author's modest claim.

The Marchioness of Yolombó integrates narrative expression, portrayal of character, and regional milieu, adding historical dimension. The picture which the novel conveys is so vast in every respect that it makes the five double-columned pages "by way of prologue" almost redundant. If one excepts the odd historical peg—for instance, the account of the founding of San Lorenzo de Yolombó and the various perplexing metamorphoses which it undergoes in the course of its existence—the substance of the prologue is reflected more colorfully, and indeed entertainingly, in the pages of the novel itself. This would seem to apply specifically to the instances of social and religious satire and to the intriguing glimpses of mundane conduct among Yolombó's ruling class.

Bárbara Caballero, the marchioness heroine, is an appealing figure. Her life spans Yolombó's history from 1750 to 1830, the transition years from colony to independence. Physical beauty is not one of her distinguishing features (and it is worth remembering that the same is true for most of Carrasquilla's female characters, in whom the plain external appearance seems to throw into bolder relief their inner qualities). Bárbara's talents are manifold, and good luck is with her wherever she goes. Her dynamic personality is indefatigable. When the mining operations do not satisfy her any more, she fearlessly invades the male domain of education, laboriously learning to read and write and dedicating part of her inexhaustible energies to the founding of schools in the district. The male population is more than a little perplexed by Bárbara's revolutionary conduct, which, given the historical period, verges on blasphemy. But "Doña Perseverance" refuses to surrender to raised eyebrows. Her triumphs are material, moral, and intellectual. True, she indulges in self-worship (the same as Agustín, Juana, and Ceferino), but her "tribute to herself" issues in acts of charity and generosity.

Yet, there is one tragic flaw in this woman whose gifts have cut her out to be a leader in the community. A deeply engrained devotion to the mother country and her monarch rules all her actions, a devotion which comes close to idolatry. "Spain, mother Spain" was her motto, and the bonds which link her to the king are deeply personal ones. When Bárbara Caballero has reached the peak of her career, and Yolombó acknowledges her leadership in all fields, she suddenly finds herself haunted by a vague fear: could she be destined to die without traveling to Spain, without knowing his majesty personally? This gnawing question, becoming increasingly insistent, eventually rules her life as an obsession. The "fanatical subject" (*EPC*, II, 119), thoroughly sane in every other respect, loses all sense of proportion and moderation where Spain and her monarch are involved. When this obsessive loyalty reaches into her private life, an impostor, Fernando de Orellana, "exploits the mine" and her obsession, only to abandon her soon after. Bárbara Caballero's extravagant fanaticism, which blinds her to reality, proves her undoing, and the moment of culminating triumph, the brilliant inauguration of her new functions as marchioness,[8] ushers in her fall, as Fernando abuses her trust.

Bárbara Caballero is the most clearly defined character, with her dynamic exterior, her stirling moral virtues, and her disaster-breeding psychological weakness. The author keeps her before the reader throughout the novel, directly and indirectly, perhaps more so than any other of his major characters. Introducing her on the second page at the age of sixteen, when her gifts of character and her intellectual leanings awaken timidly, he records her death in the penultimate paragraph and lets her shadow vanish in the final sentence.

Surrounding the heroine is a vast array of colorful humanity. First there is the ruling class, embodied largely in two influential families, the Caballeros and the Morenos, joined through marriage. The administrative head of Yolombó is Bárbara's father, Pedro Caballero, the highly respected mayor of the town who administers justice with absolute integrity and without regard for political influence or family ties.

His wife Rosalía, of Andalusian origin, is described as the perfect wife of a civil servant of the period. Though her level of intelligence

does not challenge her husband's authority, she can boast never-
theless a certain degree of "culture." "She knew, after a fashion,
how to read and to sign her name" ("medio sabe leer y echar la
firma"—*EPC*, II, 23). Her strength of endurance and self-abnega-
tion are put to a continuous test by her older daughter, Luz, whom
the author describes deftly as a "living thing which bears fruit"
(*EPC*, II, 41), because her whole existence seems to be an uninterrupted string of pregnancies.

Don Vicente, Luz's husband, constitutes the link with the Moreno
family. Inclined to smile at his rotund wife's eccentricities, he turns
into a stern disciplinarian where his son Martín is concerned. As
Don Pedro's logical successor in office, he feels that he cannot
dismiss his son's irresponsible conduct as merely youthful pranks.

Martín himself, the only issue on which grandfather and father
do not see eye to eye, is simply overwhelming. His irrepressible
vitality, endowed as he is "with an angel's face and a devil's heart"
(*EPC*, II, 114), assure him of extreme popularity in the village and
of almost legendary fame in some quarters. If the author had been
intent upon proving a point of literary determinism, Martín would
have easily escaped all responsibility in matters regarding the fair
sex. His Don-Juanesque leanings seem to lead straight back to his
paternal grandfather José María Moreno, affectionately nicknamed
"Good Old Moreno," one of the most lovable and vibrantly human
characters in the novel. His pride in his native city Seville is proverbial, his personal conduct more human than exemplary. "I can't
sleep alone," he confesses, "because I feel very cold" ("no puedo
dormir solo porque me da mucho frío"—*EPC*, II, 46). (Carrasquilla
may well have had this delightful "old reprobate" in mind when,
in the prologue to the novel, he refers to the "notorious exploits"
of the Moreno family.)

The regional milieu surrounding the principals is composed of
miners, peasants, workers, and domestics, representing the colonial
melting pot of Indians, Spaniards, and Negroes, Criollos, Mestizos,
and Mulattoes. The novel, however, while intensely conscious of
local color and its important function in endowing the narrative with
authenticity, never focuses on the shapeless mass.[9] Carrasquilla
takes great pains to individualize even his secondary characters. We
need but think of Bárbara's niece Antonina, whose personal frustration prompts her unsavory behavior toward her respected aunt;
Liboria Layos, who initiates Bárbara into the wonders of the al-

phabet; as well as Sacramento and Guadalupe, Bárbara's trusted
Negro servants.

Equally varied are the themes introduced relating to the political,
economic, social, religious, and intellectual texture of the period.
Some are decorative in nature and merely serve purposes of local
color. Most of them are organically linked to the major events in
the story.

Spiritual manifestations receive due emphasis, since the supernatural forms an integral part of the people's lives, affecting rulers
and ruled alike. In the discussion of religious practices of the pop-
ulace, Carrasquilla may indulgently smile at certain superstitions
and perhaps at the faithful parishioners who occasionally doze off
while the priest is saying mass. But on the whole, Carrasquilla does
not ridicule those practices, because his sympathies are with the
good old days when the rhythm of life still left room for "spontaneity
and humor," traits which our modern artificialities have all but
destroyed (*EPC*, II, 63).

The Marchioness of Yolombó is easily the author's most elaborate
novel, involving the public and private concerns of Carrasquilla's
ancestors,[10] though he claims to have made minor changes to suit
his literary purpose. He succeeds in capturing a piece of colonial
history in all its vitality. Even more than in *The Blue-eyed Boy*, the
milieu is thoroughly integrated. While it would be easy to isolate
cuadros and even *cuentos*, both supernatural and contemporary (the
extreme realism of Good Friday proceedings resulting in the death
of a Negro servant could be one of the latter), there is no doubt
that Carrasquilla at this mature stage of his career weaves characters,
historical background, and contemporary local milieu into one organic whole. In this vast canvas there is an unforgettable human
being, whose dreams and frustrations the author probes inexorably.
Her decay reflects the decadence in colonial rule. She is one of the
most attractive characters in Spanish American letters,[11] both a
psychological and a literary triumph. The novel as a whole fits
Lubbock's apt description of *War and Peace*, for it is "crowded with
life, at whatever point we face it."[12] It serves as a worthy introduction to the *Long Ago* trilogy.

IV   Long Ago

At first sight, Carrasquilla's "swan song" has much in common
with former works, both short and long. The author indulges in

reminiscences: once more a little boy represents the focal point of his attention and once again the boy's destinies are guided by a loyal factotum. The echoes of theme, incident, and treatment seem to extend from "Simon Magus" through *A Child's Heart* to *The Blue-eyed Boy*, in all of which the author captures childhood from the vantage point of age, allowing himself that refreshing "bath of innocence" (*EPC*, II, 612).

A closer look, however, reveals the important points of difference between the reminiscences which sporadically occur throughout Carrasquilla's long life and Eloy Gamboa's memoirs, which by virtue of their maturity take their rightful place beside *The Marchioness of Yolombó*. Both, I submit, are equally climactic to Carrasquilla's literary work. Both are the author's eloquent tribute to Antioquia's past, though different periods in the region's history are under scrutiny. Since *Long Ago* deals with an era less "long ago" than *The Marchioness of Yolombó*, Carrasquilla's appraisal of local conditions is bound to be less conjectural in the former than in the latter, where he is compelled to rely on other peopel's eyewitness accounts. Finally, *Long Ago* involves documentation by expert informants.[13]

The autobiographical medium which earlier works apply to more restricted spans of time now enables the author to evoke an entire period in his region's annals and to explore the factors which shape a personality. Carrasquilla does not forgo his spontaneity and his powers of observation, which keep him close to the heartbeat of his people's traditions and colorful speech. The intimately local story achieves universal scope through its psychological overtones, its subtle human shading, and its breadth of vision.

It is interesting to note that Carrasquilla's most mature pages of recollection stem from the days when he is all but immobilized and confined to a wheelchair "like my hero Dimitas Arias" "(*EPC*, II, 802). The same as Sarmiento, who produces the most poignant pages of interpretation of his native Argentina far away from the scene of events, Carrasquilla in *Long Ago* does not copy directly from nature but evokes the setting and the human essence of days gone by, filtered through a discriminating mind and a mature aesthetic, ripened by distance not only in time but also in space.

The plot in Carrasquilla's last novel reflects what Lubbock describes as "one of the oldest and most universal ones . . . that of the journey."[14] The mining milieu makes for an atmosphere which, with its emphasis on material detail, tends to undermine not only the language but frequently the moral fiber of those who pursue the hazardous dance of gold. In terms of education, this means that young Eloy Gamboa is restricted in his freedom of movement, which in turn means that the initial growth of his personality is linked largely to the home.

His first conscious contact with the physical universe occurs when the family changes its living quarters. His earliest impressions beyond the shelter of the home are clearly negative, and a little frustrating, because they clash with some of his most precious illusions. The river, far from being crystalline, displays an unattractive dirty shade (*EPC*, II, 232); the process of diving is not at all what he imagined it to be. Also, the moral sphere brings disillusioning experiences. Not only is he repelled by human cruelty, which he identifies with the hunters returning triumphantly with their prey "suspended from a stick," but he also comes face to face with the unsavory practices of a consummate hypocrite. The dramatic clash between the man who poses as village benefactor and staunch Cantalicia, who strips him of his mask, has superficial points of similarity with Irene Carba's defiant challenge of Don Ceferino (in "Superman") and particularly with Rumalda's dauntless intervention on behalf of her foster child in *The Blue-eyed Boy*. For young Eloy, the violent encounter is anything but entertaining. It constitutes his first direct contact with the most insidious form of hypocrisy, and as such, it is profoundly depressing. But perhaps the most shocking aspect of the episode is the knowledge that his own father has brought all this upon himself through his greed and his gambling mentality. Mining here has turned into an obsession which spells total failure.

But Eloy's personal ledger also records credit entries. The latter relate largely to three figures who prominently shape the introductory phase in his young life, which is examined in Volume One of the trilogy, entitled *Among Rivers and Rocks (Por aguas y pedregones)*. I am referring to his mother, Rosita Gallego, as well as to Cantalicia and Nicanor—three "mentor" influences in *Long Ago*.

Rosita is one of those sensitive mother figures who clearly reveal autobiographical flavor. First sketched in "Simon Magus" and "Blanca," she appears in clear focus in *A Child's Heart* and finally, fully developed, in *Long Ago*. Eloy's relationship to his mother reflects an attractive spectrum of subtle human touches, displaying the growth of his aesthetic sensitivity. Eloy, the same as Paco some thirty years before, is deeply impressed with his mother. (In *Long Ago*, there is no saintly grandmother to divert attention.) When Eloy is presented with the dog Canelo, he admits looking at the dog and then at his mother, wondering "which of the two appeared more beautiful to him" (*EPC*, II, 218). Some time later, when his mother is recovering from an illness, the boy allows his eyes to wander from the Virgin statue to his mother and confesses that the two seem very·similar.

The impressions which crowd the child's imagination at this stage are so chaotic that he tries in vain to impose some semblance of order. He has gathered up many facts in terms of intellectual learning (and in this respect the autobiographical element certainly is less noticeable, since Carrasquilla acknowledges candidly that he never learnt anything anywhere). As yet he is unable to correlate and to coordinate those facts.

On the other hand, the moral and spiritual spheres prove more of a problem for Eloy, who has to feel his way around with caution. His somewhat nebulous contact with death assumes concrete dimensions when his mother and father die in rapid succession. At this point his two guardian angels, Cantalicia and Nicanor Builes, come into full play. The latter is a jack of all trades who is devoted to the child and always willing (and usually able) to satisfy his curiosity with respect to the native milieu and its simple inhabitants, their work, and their entertainment. Nicanor proves a mine of information and a significant supplement to the boy's isolated and often chance observations and impressions. Cantalicia, the faithful servant of Indian origin, is so deeply attached to the boy that she threatens dire retribution to anyone who would dare touch him. Her sinister threats are never put to a test, but Eloy's mother, who knows Cantalicia best, suggests that her bark is decidely more fierce than her bite since her tender heart would preclude violence even toward a rabid dog (*EPC*, II, 213). The personality of Cantalicia, her sterling character and her social station, bring to mind the ingenuous Negro servant Frutos of "Simon Magus," whose overwhelming affection leads to undesirable consequences. Frutos is a sketch for Cantalicia, though the short story imposes restrictions in the portrayal of character where the novel permits elaboration.

The boy's moral awakening, which is paramount in the first volume of *Long Ago*, becomes subordinate to his spiritual growth in the second part, entitled *Amidst Peaks and Ravines (Por cumbres y cañadas).* After Eloy has taken leave of Cantalicia and Nicanor to follow "the road into the unknown" (*EPC*, II, 334), he is in short order sucked up by a whirlpool of fresh impressions and sensations which surround him in his new milieu.

At the beginning of the second part, Eloy is twelve years old. The year 1871 is mentioned as the year of "my arrival" at the mine (*EPC*, II, 394), which corresponds to the author's biography. The narrative in this second part of the novel has greater scope and variety than that of the first part. The obvious reason is that, as the boy's moral and, above all, his intellectual vision widens, the vague and superficial answers do not suffice, and a more thorough evaluation of the problems of the physical and moral universe becomes indicated. The wealth of detail is coupled with a greater variety of incident and characters whose conversations open up a wondrous new world to Eloy. In the second part of the novel, the matter of education comes to the fore. Miguel and Elisa Moncada have formally taken the place of Eloy's parents, but Eloy's "Virgil" is their son Teodorete, who becomes the boy's constant companion and who, just as Nicanor Builes before him, assumes the mentor role, doing his best to satisfy the boy's curiosity.

In this second volume, Eloy shows a peculiar dualism. Longing to become equally accomplished in the intellectual and physical spheres ("I want to work," he explains, adding quickly that he also wishes to study "to become a doctor"—*EPC*, II, 355), he soon becomes sadly disillusioned. In the realm of formal learning he makes rapid strides, but in that of physical endeavor, the efforts expended usually prove disproportionate to the results achieved. Despite his foster mother's comforting assurances that his main concern should be his education, his ineptness at physical labor depresses little Eloy. Here is a basic difference between Paco, Regina, Ligia, Juan de la Rosa on one side, and Eloy Gamboa on the other. Though Eloy's failure to adjust to his surroundings inevitably results in a certain isolation from the remainder of his age group, he never experiences the sense of superiority which set the others aside from their environment. On the contrary, Eloy always appears intent upon correcting what he regards as a shortcoming.

As the discussions focus on the problem of education, Carrasquilla over and over again points to women as the ideal educators of the young and as the obvious trustees of culture in mining regions. In the Moncada household, to cite an example, Don Miguel is a self-made man who has acquired a mastery in his architectural profession "without either eating or drinking it" (*EPC*, II, 367). But in the cultural realm, his wife Elisa's authority is unquestioned: she reads "forbidden books" and, having picked up her pen, is loath to put it down.

Aesthetic impressions form an important part of Eloy's intellectual development. Music, for instance, which up to that point has been a spiritual experience connected exclusively with church visits and ceremonies, now enters his life as an autonomous aesthetic sensation, without spiritual connotation. Eloy is unable to define his reaction in concrete terms; he merely confesses that he is "beside himself" (*EPC*, II, 369) while listening to folk music with guitar accompaniment.

The parallel situations which occur in Volumes I and II of the novel conceal, as so often in Carrasquilla's literary art, subtle changes under a deceptively simple exterior. Eloy's relationship to his foster mother Elisa is a case in point. We cannot help recalling two revealing episodes in Part I: When Eloy's eyes wander from his mother to his new dog Canelo, he wonders which of the two is more attractive; at a later point, he is struck with the resemblance between his mother and the Virgin. Now Eloy has grown beyond the externals, and the spontaneous, delightfully naive confessions of Part I have been enriched by a new sensation: an aural one. Listening to his foster mother's voice leaves the boy with a lasting emotional impression; outwardly, he adds candidly, "she does not seem beautiful" (*EPC*, II, 337).

Teodorete not only emulates Virgil in guiding Eloy intellectually but at one point leads him through the "underworld" during a visit to the mine (which apparently impresses Eloy as little as it did Carrasquilla, according to his letter from Sanandrés). His eighteen year old brother Martiniano—Marto for short—provides a more immediate, though superficial, attraction because of his dazzling oratory. Marto's "spectacular erudition," which consists largely of parroting a vast number of titles of books which he has never opened, brings to mind Don Ceferino's hollow ministry in Minerva's temple. The "Superman" story, which appeared in 1920 as one of the aquarels (see Chapter 5), recurs in the second volume of *Long Ago*, signaling Marto's triumphant return to the village from which he fled earlier. Despite his spectacular protest against Don Ceferino's teaching methods and the all too ready strap, Marto and his teacher subscribe to the same motto: "I don't understand, but I always talk" ("no entiendo, pero siempre digo"—*EPC*, II, 432).

Flanked by Teodoro and later by Martiniano, Eloy matures in a picturesque setting which abounds in universal human detail. Without singling out any of the colorful figures, it is evident that the human environment which plays a more or less immediate part in Eloy's growth is endowed with more variety and more individuality in this phase of Eloy's life than in the one portrayed in the first volume of the novel. Besides, such violent plot devices as Melchorita's assassination are replaced in Part II by humble details of Antioqueño life and popular dialogue which surround the spiritual and aesthetic growth of a young boy.

Part III witnesses the most radical changes in Eloy's affairs. Entitled *From the Country to the City (Del campo a la ciudad)*, or *From the Mountain to the City (Del monte a la ciudad)*,[15] it focuses on the most mature section in the boy's reminiscences, recording his mental and intellectual growth. It develops against a divided background, since, two-thirds through the volume, young Eloy bids farewell to the "symphony of gold that never ceases" (*EPC*, II, 526) and to his childhood, moving to Medellín for his higher education.

The section in Part III devoted to the country setting involves largely the characters of Parts I and II, mainly the latter, and constant thematic echoes of the preceding pages. However, the boy's mental attitude has changed, with spontaneous reaction yielding to intellectual scrutiny. The mine, for example, which he spontaneously rejected after his first "descent" in Part II, now turns into the object of intellectual curiosity, and he approaches its technical details with an open mind. A similarly open mind enables Eloy now to seek the essential nature of things and of people and to savor a spiritual essence despite an unattractive exterior. The bishop's visit (which has clear autobiographical echoes if we think of Carrasquilla's letter from Sanandrés in 1907) is an interesting illustration of this point.

In portraying Medellín of the eighteen seventies, with its political, social, economic, and intellectual details, Carrasquilla once more taps his phenomenal memory, though Eloy Gamboa (unlike the author himself) decides to return to his law books after the civil war in 1876. The novel ends happily,[16] as Eloy, after receiving his law and political science degrees and entering into partnership with his old friend Teodoro, remembers another "old friend" in marrying his childhood sweetheart Elenita.

The *Long Ago* trilogy closes with an epilogue outlining the later lives of its principal characters and concluding upon a profession of faith by the almost eighty year old author, who states without hesitation that "the upsets of the present do not upset me . . . I see in them . . . the thirst for the eternal which moves mankind" ("las inquietudes de la actualidad no me inquietan . . . veo en ellas . . . la sed de lo eterno que mueve a la humanidad"—*EPC*, II, 560).

With this deeply personal credo, Carrasquilla bids farewell to his readers and to his literary career. His valedictory is his most ambitious piece of writing and a worthy companion piece to *The Marchioness of Yolombó*. Structurally, he appears to have striven for balance among the three parts, which are of almost equal length.[17] The perfect integration of narrative, psychological probing, and background which begins with *The Blue-eyed Boy* reaches complete fruition in *The Marchioness of Yolombó* and the first two volumes of *Long Ago*.

The third volume, in my view, lacks the artistic unity and the spontaneous charm of the two others and is clearly anticlimactic. Its flaws become particularly marked during the final part, which takes place in Medellín and which dispenses entirely with one of the most effective elements of the author's literary art, dialogue. Here the human immediacy which is Carrasquilla's most telling claim to immortality is absent. The bird's eye view of Medellín in the eighteen seventies assumes dimensions totally disproportionate to the boy whose growth has made the other two volumes so fascinatingly human. The "circumstances of time and place" prevail over those of "person" (*EPC*, II, 526), and the cultural and political backgrounds tend to smother Eloy's living humanity.

Federico de Onís affirms that *Long Ago*—least novelistic among all of Carrasquilla's novels[18]—sums up par excellence the author's art. I am inclined to agree, with the aforementioned reservations. The homely regional details, the lively authentic speech, the living characters, and the patient probing of a child's heart and mind turn *Long Ago*, if not into the culminating work of the writer's career, at least into his most typical piece of writing.

Carrasquilla is at his finest when he drinks from the "profound spring of humble humanity." This, I submit, he does most effectively in *The Blue-eyed Boy*, *The Marchioness of Yolombó*, and Parts I and II of *Long Ago*.

CHAPTER 7

The Newspaper Columnist
(1914–1919)

CARRASQUILLA'S caustic words of pseudoconfession, "I write because they pay me,"[1] sound unconvincing because they do not reflect the man's human and aesthetic philosophy. Federico de Onís as usual hits the nail on the head: Carrasquilla wrote simply because he could not do otherwise. He was a born writer.

One section, however, among the author's writings comes into being doubtless because they paid him for it—namely, the chronicle or sketch of customs, succinct glimpses in which the background or moral commentary, local or universal in nature, overshadow the living individual. It is this type of writing which I have deliberately disregarded in the last three chapters in studying Carrasquilla's growth as a creative artist and analyzing the salient features of his literary production.

For the sake of the fleeting moments of personal confession which occur in these brief pieces and which might supplement our understanding of the human being, let us now turn to the "Native Chronicler" (to use the name of the newspaper column to which Carrasquilla contributed). His activities in this area can be isolated without much difficulty, since they are tied in the main to the five year span between 1914 and 1919—toward the end of Carrasquilla's second creative period—and fall into three broad chronological divisions: (1) the pre-Bogotá phase, which comprises chiefly the sketches written in 1914 and published later under the collective title of *Sunday Sketches (Dominicales)*, closest in character to his short stories; (2) the few pieces which have their origin during the five years in Bogotá; and finally, (3) the post-Bogotá phase, from which the fourteen "Medellín" sketches stand out.

I   *The Pre-Bogotá Period*

During the months preceding his second trip, Carrasquilla published chronicles and sketches dealing with various aspects of the
regional setting, censuring social foibles and in general singling out
for examination local problems or institutions which captured his
artistic or human imagination.[2]

One such institution, depicted under the title "Bees" ("Abejas"),
was the work done by girls from wealthy homes who dedicated
themselves to caring for Medellín's poor. "Like bees, they fly away
from the hive and return laden with the supplies which their hon-
eycomb requires" ("Como las abejas, se escapan de la colmena, para
tornar a ella provistas de los materiales que su panal requiere"—
EPC, I, 701). Genuine admiration for those "bees of the divine
hive" prompted Carrasquilla's words of homage to their works of
charity.

The secluded retreat of San Miguel de los Angeles, described in
the chronicle "Hermitage" ("Ermita"), was another such institution
which filled a spiritual need in the community. In the care of its
aged chaplain, it breathed poetry by virtue of its very simplicity.
Carrasquilla's sensitive response to its serene atmosphere foreshadowed the chronicle "Souls" ("Almas") with its unmistakable
"tribute of envy" to the Carmelite convent, its shady graveyard, its
flowers, and the flocks of humble birds gathering at dusk.

Medellín's public gardens, and particularly the beautiful Bolívar
Park, come under scrutiny in "Lycea" ("Liceos"). They are ideal
spots for those who wish to commune with themselves or with
others and most appropriate for young people, who crave a moment's privacy away from mother's watchful eye. In defending parks
against the few who object on moral grounds, Carrasquilla suggests
a common sense solution. Let parents express their concern by
instilling into their daughters a balanced sense of values, he recommends; the rest will take care of itself. The moral question which
is implicit in the discussion of the place of public parks in Medellín's
social life lends a broad application to a restricted local phenomenon.

"Hail, oh Common Man" ("¡Ave, oh vulgo!") is a hymn to
Medellín's suburbs, where life adheres to its spontaneous "natural
rhythm" (*EPC*, I, 684), the most rewarding milieu for the sociologist
as well as for the lay observer. It is in suburbia where Carrasquilla
detects American democracy at its purest, because here common

people live untrammeled by convention and artifice. "Hail, oh Common Man" reaffirms, in the unspoiled setting of Medellín's outskirts, the author's conviction that "our aristocracy can only issue from the union between intelligence and will" ("nuestra aristocracia sólo puede resultar de la unión de la inteligencia y de la voluntad"— *EPC*, I, 684) and his insistence upon everyday occurrences as his most rewarding literary raw material. "Titans" ("Titanes"), the chronicle of indefatigable Petrona, an "epic of work" incarnate, provides further proof that Carrasquilla considers honest work "the most illustrious pedigree."[3]

On June 17, 1914, Carrasquilla published the second[4] in a set of sketches which in 1934 were to reappear under the collective title of "Sunday Sketches." Continuing to scrutinize his fellow humans in their "essential nature," and focusing on their Sunday pursuits, Carrasquilla depicted typical experiences by typical people.

"Peasants" ("Campesinos") is a genuine sketch of customs, which portrays a Sunday in the Antioqueño countryside and deals with a local family boasting nine children and twenty-seven grandchildren. Sunday for them is a busy day combining the spiritual with the secular, worship closely joined to business transactions, and culminating in the customary retreat of old Anselmo and his wife, in time-honored seclusion remote from noisy children and screaming grandchildren.

After portraying the typical country scene, Carrasquilla focused on a typical student dilemma. The sketch entitled "Students" ("Estudiantes") provides a biting commentary on a failing which is as widespread among students as it is lamentable to their professors—namely, that of carousing in the company of kindred souls instead of preparing for the final examinations. The author's satire addressed itself to a common human type, ruled by vanity, who throws all prudence to the winds when his position among his peers is concerned. There is some autobiographical flavor in "superman" Juaco, who tries so hard to outshine his companions that his most valued possessions end up in the pawn shop.

"Balsam for the Spirit" ("Curas de almas") poses a spiritual problem. Father Gil, overwhelmed by the irony of his ministry, has come to question his vocation. Yearning to live near God and to share ineffable blessings, he has been forced into perpetual contact with human misery and with persons whom he despises. The Sunday which the reader witnesses throws his conflict into relief—on one hand his rotten surroundings, on the other his failure to provide urgently needed ministry. Searching his conscience, he suspects pride at the root of his actions, and the most punctilious observance of the ritual does not remove the nagging doubt about his vocation. Father Gil's mystical leanings, "more heart than head" (*EPC*, II, 573) echo Blanca's fervor (see Chapter 4) and foreshadow the elemental sincerity of Rogelio's spontaneous faith (see Chapter 6).

The "rigorously historical" pact between the saintly parish priest and the troupial (depicted in "Salutaris Hostia") was followed by two hard-hitting indictments of shallow vanity, appropriately leading to frustration rather than triumph. Ina Torralba ("Dandies"— "Elegantes") loses her beau because she has turned into a paper doll, so exclusively concerned with decorative detail that she forgets to be a human being; Lolo Arellano ("Brand New"—"Estrenos") forfeits his well-earned scholastic triumph when he permits his pride to get the better of him. Instead of dazzling his environment with a pair of brand new shoes, the boy finds himself with a splitting headache and a ruined Sunday attire, indeed a frustrating balance of a promising day.

"A Memorable Sunday" ("Veinticinco reales de gusto") contains, in the form of Graciela's climactic disgrace coupled with her spoiled gala outfit, faint echoes of Lolo's embarrassing experience. Besides, the sketch offers one more glimpse of average people in a very average situation. He is a bookkeeper of about fifty, she is forty-four: their marital life provides a model of calm stability reminiscent of the serene protagonists in "Philosophic Tranquility." The two, thoroughly set in their ways, are accustomed to doing the same things at the same time, treating themselves to a family outing once every three months. The focal point of the present sketch is one such "memorable" Sunday picnic during which the family members are joined by Graciela, a vivacious seamstress of mature age, and Fidel, an excitable engineering student of twenty. Graciela's embarrassing mishap injects the only jarring note into this rustic idyll, which unrolls in the local setting with the homely details of food, attire, and behavior. It succeeds in upsetting but momentarily the delightful serenity that has characterized the unobtrusive couple all their lives.

"Buttons and Bows" ("Vestes y moños") once more broaches the problem of spiritual sterility and the failure of shallow people to come to grips with fundamental values. The day of first communion in the home of a wealthy family reflects the discrepancy between the spiritual significance of the event and the meaning which the chief protagonists ascribe to it. The children's mother is strongly reminiscent of Doña Juana in *Grandeur*, exclusively concerned with making the celebrations conform to the standard customary in families of their social status. The children understandably find it difficult to raise their sights beyond the presents they may expect. As a sum total, life's "happiest day" turns into a sad disappointment for everyone concerned and, spiritually, into a pitiful travesty.

"Miners" ("Mineros") spells out a familiar problem: "Pay on Saturday, fray on Sunday" (*EPC*, II, 569). The Sunday in the mining milieu shows no idyllic traits. Amidst the boisterous men who drown their troubles (and their pay checks) in a grand and glorious spree, Severiano, a darling Negro boy of one, becomes embroiled in a duel between a hen and a turkey buzzard and comes close to losing his life.

The situation, needless to say, bears a definite resemblance to that of "The Child of Happiness,"which was written five years later (see Chapter 5); the author goes so far as to use the same contrast between Job's suffering and the boy's vitality. However, there is one basic difference: whereas "Miners" is a sketch of customs which emphasizes the environment, "The Child of Happiness" evolves entirely around the little boy. There is more human interest in the latter, more regional picturesqueness in the former.

The Sunday in the mine was followed by another glimpse of Medellín. Ramón Sila ("Roaming Around"—"Vagabundos") has seen better days, but life appears to have passed him by. All but abandoned by the many good friends who were not slow to help him spend his money, he now roams the streets and taverns of Medellín, vainly searching for one understanding smile. Perhaps the local color of the Medellín environment is the most living trait of this sketch, because the itinerary which the vagabond follows in his futile search for that one spark of humanity (beginning with the famous "Blumen" tavern) reminds one of Carrasquilla's favorite habit of pubcrawling which played a particularly prominent role during this period of his life.

"Mystic Ecstasy" ("Alma") depicts a woman's spiritual experience. Her ecstatic craving and the humble abode, imbued with the "intimate mystery of a church," bring to mind "Balsam for the Spirit" and foreshadow both "The Plant" and "Rogelio." The sketch is one more reminder of that spontaneous spiritual union which evoked Carrasquilla's wholehearted admiration.

The sketch "Cheers!" ("Copas") merits note chiefly because of its autobiographical reflections on the vital role of childhood reminiscences, a refreshing "bath in innocence." The somewhat abrupt regeneration of a young reprobate has distinct echoes of the unexpected penitence of Francisco Vera, while the repeated libations of the two interlocutors bring to mind similar narrative stimuli in the gaucho version of *Faust*, colorfully portrayed by the Argentine poet Estanislao del Campo, as well as the sketch entitled "One Bottle of Brandy and One of Gin" ("Una botella de Brandy y otra de Ginebra") by the Colombian satirist Emiro Kastos.

"The Gallows" ("La horca") features a young firebrand, Marcos Ciro, the eleven year old leader of a gang of boys, a noisy prankster who keeps the village constantly on edge. But once again, the chief emphasis in this sketch is not on the boy himself, but rather on the color of the milieu, particularly the "explosive" execution of the realistic Judas figure on Easter Sunday.

In all these glimpses, the human being is sketched succinctly while the colorful setting or the moral problem receive major emphasis.

II *The Bogotá Period*

In September 1914 the author went to Bogotá, and the geographic change was accompanied by a change in literary flavor. The Bogotá atmosphere clearly did not strike a responsive chord in Carrasquilla's heart, and we need but look at his correspondence to confirm this impression.

His second stay in the capital prompted a handful of chronicles beginning with the salute "Hail, oh Capital City" ("Ave, oh Urbe Capitolino"), published one month after his arrival, and ending on an apostrophe to the same city in December 1915. All the pieces from this period show essay flavor. Clearly the author was more concerned with indulging in philosophical reflections than with creating a living atmosphere with local attributes.

The initial Bogotá composition "Hail, oh Capital City" prepares us for this change in approach. It is devoid of the color enlivening the Medellín sketches and, on the whole, limits itself to a concise appraisal of his new milieu which, true to its eagle emblem, joins beauty to austerity.

The latter quality is reflected in the shade of grey—"in all its nuances"—which Carrasquilla associates with the capital city ("Grey"—"Gris") and which comes to life in the people, who seem to be perpetually in mourning. They are dressed in black, observes Carrasquilla, but laugh and joke, seemingly unmindful of the "funeral procession" which they enact.

Resplendent nature, at this point of the author's career, proves little more than a pretext for a discussion of moral and spiritual issues. This is brought out in "Brooms" ("Escobas"), in which an old man, nauseated with his surroundings, with life, and with himself, yearns for the "supreme broom" to intervene and make a clean sweep.

"Flowers" ("Flores") pays sensitive tribute to the feminine heart; "Smoke" ("Humo") to the irresistible role of Saint Nicotine in human affairs. Music comes to the fore in two chronicles with essay flavor which do honor to musicians for their contributions to Colombian folk music: the pianist Alberto Castillo for reviving a traditional Antioqueño tune ("Resurrection"—"Resurrección") and the composer Emilio Murillo, "Shakespeare of the bambuco,"[5] for revealing essential values of the national cultural heritage ("Patriotism"—"Pro Patria").

The author's reflections on philosophy and folk music were followed by an essay which, under the deceptive title "Praise of the Prudent Widow" ("Elogio de la viuda sabia"), tackled the vital role of illusion in human affairs, concluding on the familiar thesis that truth is what we believe it to be.

Next came an essay with the intriguing name "Venenete," which joined philosophy and philology in tracing the derivation of a linguistic fad in Bogotá circles. The author describes it as vast in semantic scope, with physical as well as psychological ramifications and not necessarily linked to external beauty. An English equivalent for this mysterious, widespread brand of "poison" to which Carrasquilla assigns a prominent role in aesthetics and human relations may well be "To have IT." Using as his point of departure a linguistic phenomenon in vogue in the capital, the author reflects caustically on human nature.

Finally, Carrasquilla addressed the most direct apostrophe to the capital in a chronicle entitled "December" ("Diciembre") which, with more external detail than is usual during the Bogotá period, depicts the Christmas season of 1915 in the Colombian capital. This final Bogotá chronicle is intimately linked to Carrasquilla's work in general as well as to his personality. In atmosphere it evokes "The Toy Gun," which dates from the same year and which shows how an insignificant gift can transform two lives. On the other hand, "December" lays bare once again that spiritual hunger of Carrasquilla's which disguises itself under such candid words as "this mischievousness which covers us is, in essence, the most genuine innocence" ("esta malicia que nos arropa es, en el fondo, la inocencia más genuina"—*EPC*, I, 715).

The Bogotá period came to a literary close at the end of 1915. The years from 1916 to 1918 appear to have produced no evidence either in the prose fiction or in the chronicle fields. There are only the colorful letters to his family with satirical asides and picaresque digressions which tend to reflect the human being with greater spontaneity and immediacy than do the chronicles and sketches that have been examined in this chapter. But, on the whole, Bogotá must be regarded as an arid period in terms of creativity.

III   *The Post-Bogotá Period*

Carrasquilla's return to Antioquia in 1919 sparked literary vitality anew. He published a set of chronicles paying tribute to a city which he knew thoroughly and which he admired.[6] Beginning[7] with a hymn to the magic of its natural setting and its untiring inhabitants, Carrasquilla paints an attractive picture, chock-full of local detail, calling attention not to the opulent summer homes of the rich but to the modest dwellings of the simple folk who water their earth with the sweat of their brow. Here is the true nobility as he sees it, an aristocracy based on the individual's worth and not on the accident of birth.

In his fourteen sketches entitled "Medellín," Carrasquilla brings to life such important traits as the beautiful surroundings, the capricious natural setting, the hardworking Antioqueño peasant, the prolific woman, the aristocracy of work, and the marked business acumen of the region. He shows the contrast between the hustle and bustle of the city and repose of the country, conveys the spell of a humble river "working in silence and obscurity" (*EPC*, I, 780),

and reflects on the dubious blessings of civilization as he scrutinizes old and new suburbs. In evoking the upper and lower ravines, Carrasquilla "inserts" a middle ravine of his own coinage. There is a touch of melancholy in the closing words as he laments the fact that the imposing upper ravine is no longer in use.

The vantage point of the Hill of the Crosses, which permits the observer both an analytical and a synthetic view of Medellín, reveals the roads leading in and out of the city as well as Medellín's wildly confusing street pattern. The latter is for Carrasquilla further proof of the chaos-breeding tradition of individual autonomy, which is typical of the entire area and which defies all principles of town planning and common sense. Comments on the public park system are coupled with the author's eloquent plea not to tamper with beauty and to respect sovereign nature, upon which human ingenuity cannot improve. (Medellín's public gardens here provide the opportunity for reaffirming his favorite thesis that nature is more beautiful than art.)

After a glimpse of the public squares which offers the customary mixture of geographic authenticity and moral or historical reflections, often satirical in flavor, Medellín's places of worship, traditional and more recent, come under review. Finally, there is a refreshing tribute to the waterways which traverse the city and which provide the author with a springboard for discussing the role of water in human relations.

In sum, the sketches entitled "Medellín" breathe authenticity bred by direct contact. They reflect what the Bogotá items lack on the whole—namely, that genuine understanding of, and sympathy with, his milieu which produce Carrasquilla's most effective writing. The names of regional sites evoke not only affectionate memories, but social and philosophical comments interspersed with satirical asides.

It is quite obvious that the keen observer takes up his position close enough to his geographical subject to be conscious of its detail, yet far enough not to allow this detail to blur the overall perspective. Thus he achieves—not unlike the observer who selects the vantage point of the Hill of the Crosses overlooking the city of Medellín— both geographic analysis and moral synthesis.

A few short stories stem from these five years, but on the whole, the "native chronicler" predominates during this period. As the author moves from the colorful "Sunday Sketches" through the inconsequential pieces written in Bogotá—except of course for "The Plant" and "The Toy Gun," which are anything but inconsequential—to the chronicles dedicated to Medellín, certain common traits stand out which may be said to characterize the "native chronicler" phase. Regional detail here absorbs his interest completely, and even in those cases where the human element is more pronounced (as occurs in the "Sunday Sketches"), the author usually is too intent upon underlining environmental factors or moral and social satire to pay much attention to the living being.

The predominantly social and moral focus, with frequent sallies into biting satire which is most marked during Carrasquilla's second period (see Chapter 5), weakens the living effect of the "Sunday Sketches," reducing potential short stories to sketches of customs, highly effective ones to be sure. The very same element, conversely, adds life and immediacy to the geographic flavor of the chronicles, producing a charming mixture of the general and the personal.

As has been pointed out, "native chronicler" elements are scattered all through Carrasquilla's major works, becoming increasingly intertwined and organically integrated with the human being. Antioquia is ever present in his pages, just as it is ever present in his life. The vast canvas comprises Antioqueño geography, history, customs, and institutions and is constantly enlivened by details of regional attire and cuisine and above all by the peculiarities of regional colloquial speech.

As Carrasquilla writes, Antioquia emerges in all its distinctive color: its rugged individualism, its strongly Spanish traits, its hardworking population, the inveterate controversy on its racial origin, its large, closely knit family unit, the capricious mountain setting, a regional economy based principally on mining and coffee, its educational problems, its work and leisure hours, as well as its religion, legends, and superstitions. Its dietary system still rests on what the nineteenth century poet Gregorio Gutiérrez González termed the "second trinity,"[8] namely *frijoles* (kidney beans), *mazamorra* (a very substantial corn soup), and *arepa* (corn griddle cakes), sprinkled liberally with that fragrant sugar cane beverage called *aguardiente*, both "understanding and leveling" if we are to believe Carrasquilla's expert testimony.

The "native chronicler," then, pervades the author's literary work in its entirety. But only when the native chronicler joins hands with the observer of human weakness and the master storyteller does Carrasquilla achieve maturity.

The autonomous sketches and chronicles, published between 1914 and 1919, in which the regional setting turns into an end in itself, can add but little of substance to what the novels and short stories have already told us about the author's literary craft. At best, they supplement our understanding of the human being. The newspaper columnist enlightened, and doubtless delighted, his contemporaries. But it was Carrasquilla the novelist and short story writer who addressed himself unmistakeably to posterity.

CHAPTER 8

Summing Up

A FTER a period of neglect[1] Carrasquilla is coming into his own, both in his native country and abroad. The weighty voice of Julio Cejador y Frauca, who in 1919 hailed him as "the best novelist of his country,"[2] has been joined more recently by other authoritative critics. "A writer of unique . . . worth" is Federico de Onís' definitive verdict,[3] while Carlos García Prada's label "Antioqueño classic"[4] seems to challenge the familiar definition that classics are the authors read "in class" only.

Rafael Maya exalts Carrasquilla as a "conspicuous exponent of his race and milieu,"[5] and Gerald E. Wade calls him "a truly exceptional figure in Latin American letters."[6] According to Antonio Curcio Altamar, Carrasquilla stands out as the Colombian novelist with the most extensive literary production,[7] and Arturo Torres Ríoseco predicts that posterity may well accord Carrasquilla a place above his fellow countryman José Eustasio Rivera, the author of the renowned novel *La Vorágine.*[8]

Yet Carrasquilla himself professed but scant regard for his own literary efforts. Though claiming pioneer status for one of his works,[9] he dismissed (not unlike Petrarch) his writings in general as mere trifles.

I have examined the development from "trifle" to mature masterpiece, from charming inconsequential narrative where the vision of character remains blurred, up to the moment when language, human behavior, and milieu merge to produce the most distinctive statement of the author's world. I have traced a creative curve which, though not leading uniformly upwards, reflects a gradual refinement of structural approach and literary technique. Delightful trifles occurred throughout the three creative phases, whether in the form of autonomous pieces or incorporated in longer works. Indeed, they constituted an organic part of Carrasquilla's literary vitality. But as the writer developed, the human vision which was his most lasting claim to fame burst his narrow regional moorings and reached out for universality.

Carrasquilla matured slowly. Had he died at the age of Shakespeare, Flaubert, or Dickens, many of his major works would have remained unwritten. *Grandeur, Ligia Cruz, The Blue-eyed Boy, The Marchioness of Yolombó,* and *Long Ago* came from his pen after he had passed the half century mark.

During his first creative phase, the master storyteller identified the three thematic areas which ran as *leitmotif* through his literary career: the child mind, the humble being obsessed with a single idea, and the living folklore. It was these areas which the observer of human weakness and the spokesman of a region was to explore with ever-increasing vigor and psychological depth.

"To remember is to live" was clearly Carrasquilla's motto. He enjoyed living as much as he did reminiscing. The studies of childhood, in growing complexity, occupied key positions in his development as an artist, inaugurating as well as climaxing each one of his three creative periods. Indeed, childhood confessions may be said to provide the essential pegs for an understanding of Carrasquilla's artistic growth and creative pattern. A playful childhood scene was his first literary attempt, a monumental set of recollections his valedictory. Evidently, Carrasquilla liked nothing better than to indulge in the "delirium of childhood memories" (*EPC*, II, 611).

No matter what his "point of view," whether he writes in the third person or chooses his most effective vehicle, the first person narrative (as in "Simon Magus," *A Child's Heart,* and *Long Ago*), his deep personal involvement is never in doubt. All of Carrasquilla's writings, the same as those of Goethe, are parts of a great confession.

There are a number of interesting analogies between Carrasquilla and Charles Dickens. Common to both are the colorful narrative, the psychological probing, and the searching interest in young people. Carrasquilla's literary world, like that of Dickens, can be concretely defined in regional terms. Yet their human significance transcends their geographic limitations. The two authors differ fundamentally, in that the Londoner seeks to reform his milieu, whereas the Antioqueño does not.

Michael and Mollie Hardwick describe Dickens as not "our best plotter."[10] The verdict could well be applied to Carrasquilla, though for different reasons. It may be difficult to remember the "exact twists" of Dickens' plots; it is virtually irrelevant to comment on plot in Carrasquilla. The expert storyteller with a phenomenal memory for all the trivia of everyday life was supremely unconcerned with the aspect which T.S. Eliot reserved for the "simplest auditors,"[11] namely, the plot.

This lack of concern seems to have become increasingly pronounced as his literary career progressed. In his first phase, from "Simon Magus" to *Hail, Regina*, a semblance of plot can be discerned. After that, Carrasquilla concentrates wholeheartedly on the creation of character within a picturesque milieu, and his absorbing interest in human beings all but snuffs out the details of the story. This, I submit, is the essential difference between such works as *Fruits of my Homeland* and *Long Ago*.

Carrasquilla's domain was reality, as reflected in Antioquia, its people and its landscape. As the master storyteller grew into the spokesman of a region and his human reality achieved more nuances and with it a greater degree of universal truth, his landscape, too, underwent a distinct change. Regional landscape, which started out as a backdrop and which in sketches and chronicles remained a spectator, colorful but disinterested and apart, became increasingly intertwined with the characters and closely identified with their behavior.

However, the focal point of Carrasquilla's art is the human being, particularly children and women, in a setting of everyday trivia. All of his major works refer to individuals, and bearing in mind that the *Long Ago* trilogy is subtitled *Memoirs of Eloy Gamboa*, the only two titles which do not denote explicitly female or child characters are *Fruits of my Homeland* and *Father Casafús*.

Of course, when the setting of everyday trivia encroaches upon the living being (which happens particularly during his second phase), the customs threaten to become an end in themselves. In smothering the human reactions, they weaken the overall artistic effect.

Carrasquilla's favorite and most fertile medium was the country. The city satire, whether in *Fruits of my Homeland, Grandeur,* or in numerous titles from his middle period, lent itself to a certain static quality. Consequently, some repetition marred the middle period. The tendency to repeat himself, which the spontaneous storyteller could be readily forgiven, became more of a liability when the focus was on character.

There was no sign of repetition in Carrasquilla's most mature phase. It was a period free from autonomous short pieces in which the novelist ruled supreme. This did not mean, of course, that there was less regional flavor in the final period when Carrasquilla was all but immobilized. On the contrary, if anything, the regional bond grew stronger with age. But integration took place.

The term *terruño nativo* (native soil) when used by Carrasquilla underlined his passionate conviction that, while our minds may well roam around the world in search of universal values, our hearts will always reach out for that "little corner to which affection ties us" (*EPC*, II, 53). This was basic in Carrasquilla's literary and human credo. Therefore "regionalism" in Carrasquilla's vocabulary was anything but a restrictively pejorative term. It was, on the contrary, the organic result of listening to the voice of one's heart.

Carrasquilla, it seems to me, bears an intriguing resemblance to young Tuco in "The Child of Happiness" (see Chapter 5). He is at his creative best when bubbling over with vitality, closest to his native land and its simple, unspoiled people. He loses effectiveness when theorizing and becoming embroiled in disputes and polemics. Therefore, the critic in Carrasquilla is lastingly overshadowed by the creative writer.

Many of Carrasquilla's short stories contain the substance of his longer narratives, and the latter are endowed with the charm and spontaneity of the shorter works. Both Rafael Maya and Federico de Onís agree that the spiritual kinship between long and short pieces is so intimate that their most significant difference lies in their length.[12]

But charming, uninhibited storytelling doubtless remains one of the mainstays of Carrasquilla's literary craft, and examples of this abound all through his long life. His favorite pursuit issues in colorful folk tales which draw freely on the supernatural and which are richly endowed with local attire and speech. This is magical realism at its best, and facts and characters are clearly subordinated to the delight of telling a good story.

At this point, we should ask ourselves an important question, indeed crucial for any literary creation. After reading Carrasquilla, are we likely to echo Hazlitt's tribute: "It is we who are Hamlet," or Flaubert's candid confession: "Madame Bovary, c'est moi"? In other words, do Carrasquilla's characters, who are clothed in regional attire and who express themselves in the local idiom of Antioquia, straying from standard speech in syntax and vocabulary, contain the stuff that humanity is made of? Can we identify ourselves with their feelings, their hopes and fears?

My answer must be "Yes," emphatically. At his psychological best, Carrasquilla captures the human essence and the imagination of his reader to a degree that the latter might well exclaim: "It is I who is Simon Magus, Dimas Arias, Juana Samudio, Ligia Cruz, Juan de la Rosa, Bárbara Caballero, or Eloy Gamboa."

Carrasquilla was a man whose pulsating humanity succeeded in concealing the depth of both his thinking and his emotions. He came to grips with questions of broad impact which he disguised under deceptively simple Antioqueño attire. I cannot help suspecting that underneath the rough caustic exterior which was sometimes deliberately designed to shock the bourgeois, Carrasquilla concealed a profound spiritual hunger. Mysticism intrigued him all his life, and the profession of faith which he appends to *Long Ago* is unmistakeable in its meaning. Religious themes recur in his work, and there are frequent references in his writings and correspondence which suggest to me that, almost in spite of himself, he envied those "saintly souls" nurtured by faith and love.

His life was devoted to aesthetic pursuits, and material interests were clearly secondary. He read, wrote, and conversed. His literary production, which breathed the same sincerity, simplicity, and spontaneity that characterized the pages of his uneventful life, was devoid of didacticism of any description. This was perhaps the most striking difference between him and the Spanish novelist with whom he has unjustly been compared, José María de Pereda. Pereda and Carrasquilla had only one thing in common—namely, the conviction that distinctive local values as exalted in the regional novel should remain an oasis in the "desert of modern uniformity."[13] But Carrasquilla's aesthetic orientation was wholehearted and unmarred by a political and social message, whereas Pereda could rarely resist the temptation of sermonizing. Pereda for a long time was an albatros around Carrasquilla's neck, precluding the Antioqueño novelist's just recognition. If their approach to literature was worlds apart, so was their view of life. Like Pérez Galdós, Carrasquilla might well have said: "Pereda does not doubt; I do."[14]

Little more than a century ago, Colombia made a unique con-

tribution to American letters in the form of a romantic novel which
was to become the most widely read book in Latin America—
namely, Jorge Isaacs' *María*. At a time when political and social
concerns nurtured literary endeavor, in an age of "postulants and
protestants" in the words of Arturo Uslar Pietri,[15] Isaacs' novel did
not postulate anything nor did it protest against anyone. In his
literary work, the Colombian romantic, not unlike the Spanish ren-
aissance poet Garcilaso de la Vega, shunned the turbulence of his
own life and reflected on the fleetingness of human love. The "dialogue of immortal love which was dictated by hope and cut short
by death" is alive today more than one century after its creation—
the host of editions tells the tale[16]—while other contemporary pages
have long since faded. Isaacs did permit himself the "luxury" of
being a pure artist, and so did Carrasquilla. It was to the greater
glory of their art.

It has been said that the novelist's mission is not to portray great
happenings but to endow the insignificant ones with human and
artistic interest. The "everyday happenings" of Carrasquilla (the
same as the "immortal dialogue" of Isaacs and García Márquez'
monumental enquiry into life and death) reach novelistic stature
because of their human truth and achieve greatness through their
style.

Carrasquilla's language has been hailed as one of the richest, most
varied, and most colorful of any Spanish American author. The
novelist himself postulated the supremacy of style from the outset
of his career (Chapter 3). Cejador y Frauca coupled his tribute to
Carrasquilla the stylist with a word of caution, warning the non-
Colombian writer to beware of the devices which Carrasquilla practiced with such spectacular results.[17] The successful fusion of the
literary and the popular, as well as the harmony between content
and form which Carrasquilla attained through the "difficult simplicity" of his literary technique, may well prove a hazard to would-
be imitators. Carrasquilla's "music", like that of Mark Twain, was
not for export.[18]

A remarkable canvas adorns the spacious hall of the Colombian
Academy of the Language in Bogotá. It shows many of the illustrious
character creations of the Hispanic literary heritage, both peninsular
and American. There, among Don Quixote, Sancho Panza, and Don
Juan, the gaucho Martín Fierro and the insatiable Dona Bárbara,
stands Peralta, the humble hero of our author's most renowned

cuento, "In the Right Hand of the Father," intensely Antioqueño and as irresistibly human as any of them.

Peralta, we recall (Chapter 4), found his place for eternity; Carrasquilla's niche in the literary hall of fame is equally assured. Yet there remains a significant difference between Peralta and his author. While the former became tinier and tinier, the latter is constantly growing in stature.[19]

Notes and References

Preface

1. Kurt L. Levy, *Vida y obras de Tomás Carrasquilla* (Medellín: Editorial Bedout, 1958); hereafter cited as *Vida*.
2. *Obras completas*, Edición Primer Centenario (Medellín, 1958), II, 799. The textual quotations (usually in my own English rendering) relate, unless otherwise indicated, to the First Centenary Edition of Carrasquilla's Complete Works published in 1958 by Editorial Bedout, Medellín. The abbreviation used hereafter will be *EPC* (Edición Primer Centenario), I (first volume) or II (second volume).
3. The Mexican novelist Carlos Fuentes observes that "in any society, capitalist or socialist, literature and art perform a critical task" (*Casa con dos puertas* [México, 1970] , p. 132).
4. Bernardo Arias Trujillo, author of the novel *Risaralda* (Manizales, 1935).
5. *EPC*, I, 528 ("In the Right Hand of the Father").

Chapter One

1. Joaquín Acosta,*Descubrimiento y colonización de la Nueva Granada* (Bogotá, 1942), p. 365.
2. Cervecería Unión S. A., *Monografías de Antioquia* (Medellín, 1941), p. 45.
3. Manuel Uribe Angel, *Geografía general y compendio histórico del estado de Antioquia en Colombia* (Paris, 1885), p. 644.
4. Kathleen Romoli, *Colombia, Gateway to South America* (Garden City, N.Y., 1941), p. 147.
5. Isaacs' sentimental affinity to the region was lifelong, and though not an Antioqueño by birth, he insisted on being laid to rest in a Medellín cemetery.
6. For further details of the controversy, see *Vida*, pp. 178–79.
7. Pedro Cieza de León, *La crónica del Perú*, Biblioteca de Autores Españoles (Madrid, 1862), 26, 365.
8. *Ibid.*, p. 364. (For locating the references cited in notes 7 and 8, I

am indebted to my young colleague Pedro León who devoted his doctoral dissertation to Cieza de León.)

9. Juan del Corral, in proclaiming the emancipation of the slaves in 1814, placed Antioquia in second position (following Chile) among American nations.

10. Arango, Carrasquilla, Jaramillo, Londoño, Mejía, and Restrepo (cited in alphabetical order) are just a few random samples of surnames which testify to their owner's origin.

11. Romoli, p. 148.

12. For details of the literary panorama, see my article "The Letters of Antioquia: A Dual Leitmotif," in *Revista Hispánica Moderna*, año XXXIV, núms. 3-4 (julio-octubre 1968), Homenaje a Federico de Onís, vol. II, 700–706.

13. *EPC*, II, 541.

14. For further details about Antioquia, its history, culture, and people, the reader is referred to the broadly informative volume entitled *El pueblo antioqueño* (Medellín, 1942), as well as to the section on Gregorio Gutiérrez González in Antonio Gómez Restrepo's *Historia de la literatura colombiana* (Bogotá, 1953), IV, 247–69. Truly indispensable for a knowledge of the area are the works of compilation by the late Benigno A. Gutiérrez, devoted champion of Antioqueño culture.

15. It is impossible to capture the flavor of the Spanish original "pueblo de las tres efes: feo, frío y falludo" (*EPC*, I, XXV).

16. For details relating to the novelist's genealogy, see *Vida*, p. 311.

17. Referring to his mother, Sir Winston Churchill confessed in *My Early Life: A Roving Commission* (New York, 1958): "She shone for me like the Evening Star. I loved her dearly—but at a distance" (p. 5). I suspect that Carrasquilla may have loved his father "at a distance." If the references in *A Child's Heart* are any indication, there was no distance between him and Doña Ecilda.

18. See *Vida*, p. 325.

19. This fellow student was Antonio José Restrepo, another prominent name in Antioquia's letters, whose reminiscences, "Del primer novelista antioqueño" written in 1916 (see *Prosas medulares* [Barcelona, 1929], pp. 335–48), make fascinating reading. Restrepo's colorful description of the eighteen year old Tomás has its distinct echoes in one of Carrasquilla's earliest novelistic creations, Martín Gala, the romantic protagonist in the second plot of *Fruits of my Homeland*.

20. The defeat of the rebels whom he had led was to bring Isaacs' political career to a close.

21. See *Vida*, p. 26.

22. Carrasquilla learnt his trade in the shop of Miguel Salas, a well-known tailor. One of his companions was Manuel Isaza. Both Salas and Isaza appear in Carrasquilla's earliest *crónica*, which uses as its title "El

Guarzo," a colloquial term applied affectionately to the village of El Retiro to the south of Medellín. Carrasquilla was not yet twenty when he wrote "El Guarzo."

23. There is a curious epistle written by our author on black-bordered stationery "because no other paper was available." It bears the date August 21, 1884 and is addressed to Justiniano Macía's wife Adela. The letter repeatedly refers to the "Third Story Public Library" ("Biblioteca del Tercer Piso") in Santodomingo, which according to documentary evidence did not open its doors until October 12, 1893. Besides, Macía did not reach Santodomingo until the beginning of 1889 and did not make Carrasquilla's acquaintance until a month later. Macía was married in 1891, and the above-mentioned letter testifies to a close bond of friendship between the Macía couple and Carrasquilla. The discrepancy between the date of this letter and the nature of its contents leads to the conclusion that Carrasquilla's date was ten years out and that the letter was actually written in 1894. *EPC* makes this correction without mentioning the strange slip on the original manuscript, which is in my possession (see *Vida*, p. 327).

24. See *Vida*, p. 30, for a theory about the origin of the curious name. It involved a Santodomingo youth who visited Medellín and was lodged by his relatives on the third floor of their sumptuous home. Since three story buildings were all but unknown in Santodomingo, the youngster could not get over the novel experience and, on his return, referred constantly to the "third story." Carrasquilla and Rendón might have had this amusing incident in mind when they baptized the new public library.

25. See *Vida*, p. 34.

26. Restrepo was president from 1910 to 1914.

27. Luis Flórez attributes the frequent local use of saints names with diminutive suffix to the "affectionate nature" of Antioqueños (*Habla y cultura popular en Antioquia* [Bogotá, 1957], p. 363). One of the examples which Flórez cites is "San Antoñito."

28. As I pointed out in *Vida* (pp. 38–39), various family members often vied for the privilege of providing the novelist with secretarial services.

29. Doña Susana passed away in Bogotá in 1970 shortly after her ninetieth birthday.

30. "The Toy Gun" was discovered after a lengthy search (for details see *Vida*, pp. 48–50). Whether or not *El Liberal Ilustrado*, which in its number of June 3, 1915, carried the story, actually contained its earliest publication is difficult to determine. Carrasquilla himself described "The Toy Gun" as one of his "first writings;" besides, a Christmas story would not seem appropriate for the June number of a journal. The reader cannot help wondering whether the first publication of "The Toy Gun" ties in with the *Fruits of my Homeland* period and is hidden in the Christmas issue of some journal or newspaper, possibly in Bogotá.

31. For details see *Vida*, pp. 56 ff.

32. See *Vida*, p. 61.

33. See *Vida*, p. 62.

34. The two terms cited are "Toxemia Shock" and "Artritis obliterante."

35. For further details relating to Carrasquilla's life and documentation of the facts cited, see *Vida*, ch. 1.

Chapter Two

1. The pun—a reference to the Spanish verb *tomar*(in the sense of "to drink")—is of course, untranslatable.

2. See "Hackneyed Theme" (" ema trillado"—*EPC*, II, 696–98), an essay written on the occasion of a short story contest for ladies in Medellín.

3. Though *EPC* includes the "Open Letter" among Carrasquilla's writings (II, 639 ff.) and the author himself claims to have written it "in defense of slandered innocence" (*EPC*, II, 709), it should be noted that Carlos E. Mesa attributes the same piece to the pen of Mother Laura Montoya, describing it as one of her "principal writings" (See "Laura Montoya, Escritora" in *Universidad de Antioquia*, 151 [October, November, December 1962], pp. 607–36).

4. See Levy, "Carrasquilla y la religión," in *Memoria del Sexto Congreso del Instituto Internacional de Literatura Iberoamericana* (México, 1954), pp. 213–22.

5. See "Little Saint Anthony" (*EPC*, I, 571–77).

6. See Levy, "New Light on Tomás Carrasquilla," in *Publications of the Modern Language Association of America*, LXVIII, 1 (March, 1953), 65–74.

7. Theresa, the deeply human saint of Avila, recommended this formula: "A Dios rogando y con el mazo dando."

Chapter Three

1. *EPC*, II, XIV.

2. Enrique de la Casa, *La novela antioqueña* (México, 1942), p. 45.

3. Miguel de Cervantes, "Viaje del Parnaso," *Obras completas* (Madrid, 1949), p. 66.

4. For details of the Laura Montoya episode, see Chapter 2.

5. See Max Grillo, "Contra-Homilía," published in *Alpha* (Medellín), I, no. 3 (May 1906).

6. The Spanish essayist and literary critic Benito Gerónimo Feijoo y Montenegro (1676–1764) seeks to prove his point that literary imitation is basically futile by using the graphic illustration that an ant which watches an eagle soar still remains an ant (See "El no sé qué," in *Biblioteca de Autores Españoles* [Madrid, 1883], vol. 56, pp. 349–353).

7. In his searching analysis of the two "Homilies" (which forms Sections

IX and X of his book *Los orígenes del modernismo en Colombia* [Bogotá, 1961]), Rafael Maya discusses Carrasquilla's position as a critic. He reaches the conclusion that, though Carrasquilla's opposition to some aspects of *modernismo* was uncompromising, his basic doctrines have been vindicated in the past forty years. America has witnessed the "literary 20th of July" (Colombia's Independence Day) which the Antioqueño predicted early in the century. Nigel Sylvester's interesting monograph *The "Homilies" and "Dominicales" of Tomás Carrasquilla* (University of Liverpool, Centre for Latin American Studies, 1970) unfortunately does not mention Maya's work.

8. The essay is entitled "Three Names."

9. Carrasquilla was critical of his young contemporaries in Antioquia for allowing Mejía's spontaneous tribute to his native mountains to fade, while devoting their energies to the study of foreign writers.

10. See "Autobiography" (*EPC*, I, XXVII).

11. See Ernesto González, *Cariátides* (Medellín, 1928), prologue, p. 2.

12. Carrasquilla's words "benaventear un poquito" pun on the name of the popular twentieth century Spanish playwright Jacinto Benavente, a Nobel Prize winner for drama.

13. "There's no such thing as a morally bad novel: its moral effect depends entirely on the moral quality of its reader" (Northrop Frye, *The Educated Imagination* [Bloomington, 1964], p. 94).

14. This in essence restates his familiar doctrine that the reader "recreates" the literary work, since "the beautiful and the ugly depend on the taste of the individual" (*EPC*, II, 680).

15. See the essay "Heresies" (*EPC*, II, 629–638).

16. The Peruvian literary critic Luis Alberto Sánchez shows the perplexing variety of definitions of the novel genre when citing, in the introductory chapter of *Proceso y contenido de la novela hispanoamericana* (Madrid, 1953), pp. 15–44, a cross-section of critical views, selected more or less at random and frequently conflicting.

17. Federico de Onís (*EPC*, II, XXI) has pointed to the affinity between Carrasquilla and Unamuno in their assessment, positive as well as negative, of certain tenets of *modernismo*.

18. "About a Book" ("Sobre un libro") (*EPC*, II, 699–701).

19. See "Autobiography" (*EPC*, I. XXV–XXVI).

20. *De Bogotá al Atlántico* (Paris, 1897).

Chapter Four

1. "El Guarzo" deserves mention chiefly because of its date. If the latter is accurate (as stated in *EPC*, I, 571), the author composed it when he was nineteen years old, had abandoned his law books, and had turned

temporarily to tailoring. The unpretentious story, which depicts a Sunday visit to a small village, abounds in apt descriptive detail whose caustic succinctness foreshadows the future novelist.

2. This was the only pseudonym which Carrasquilla ever used, and it was the only time that it occurred. (See Rubén Pérez Ortiz, *Seudónimos colombianos* [Bogotá, 1961], pp. 25, 166.)

3. This is the imaginative rendering suggested by Harriet de Onís' fine anthology *The Golden Land* (New York, 1948), p. 163.

4. See ch. 1, note 19.

5. Seymour Menton goes beyond the factor of mere chronology when he suggests: "If *María* enjoys the distinction of being the best romantic novel in all of Spanish America, *Frutos de mi tierra* deserves the same honor as far as the realistic movement is concerned." (Seymour Menton, "*Frutos de mi tierra o Jamones y Solomos*" Estudio Preliminar, in Tomás Carrasquilla, *Frutos de mi tierra*, p. xvi [Bogotá, 1972].)

6. I find it hard to believe that, while writing his novel, Carrasquilla could have been as oblivious as Tolstoi supposedly was of the fact that he was writing "two novels at once." See Percy Lubbock, *The Craft of Fiction* (London, 1921), p. 32.

7. Isabel Carrasquilla de Arango, *Filis y Sarito* (Medellín, no date); *Pepa Escandón* (Medellín, 1932).

8. See *Vida*, p. 144.

9. Antonio Curcio Altamar, *Evolución de la novela colombiana* (Bogotá, 1957), p. 165.

10. A Spanish card game.

11. The reference is to Tirso de Molina's seventeenth century play *El burlador de Sevilla* (*The Trickster of Seville*), in which the Don Juan character makes his triumphant entrance on the world stage.

12. A square and relatively heavy poncho: distinctive part of the Antioqueño peasant's attire, which may have a linguistic association with the French city of Rouen.

13. Death's knocking at the door of the renowned Spanish reconquest warrior Rodrigo Manrique (as recorded in the fifteenth century "Coplas" by Jorge Manrique) proved a less hazardous venture for the supernatural visitor.

14. Carrasquilla may have been thinking of one of the tales which Joseph Bédier gathered in *Les Fabliaux* (*Etudes de littérature populaire et d'histoire littéraire du Moyen Age*, 5th ed. [Paris, 1925]). However, to search for a "French original" is probably an idle pursuit, since versions of this popular theme, or variations on it, doubtless exist in the folk legacy of all languages. Bédier claims to know twenty-two variants of the tale "Quatre Souhaits Saint Martin" in which a supernatural visitor grants a number of wishes (p. 213). The reader who wishes to pursue the subject

of sources may consult, besides Bédier's exhaustive study, such indispensable works of reference as Stith Thompson, *Motif Index of Folk Literature* (Bloomington, 1932–36); D.P. Rotunda, *The Motif Index of the Italian Novella in Prose* (Bloomington, 1942); and Stith Thompson and Jonas Balys, *The Oral Tales of India* (Bloomington, 1958). Stith Thompson's overall plan and classification are adopted in all these works. Such specific categories as "Magic Powers and Manifestations," "Rewards and Punishments" and, above all, "Deception by Disguise or Illusion" offer much relevant material, drawn from oriental and other sources. Rosa María Lida's informative *El cuento popular hispanoamericano y la literatura* (Buenos Aires, 1941) examines specifically the Spanish American folk *cuento* within the context of the European literary tradition. None of the themes treated by Carrasquilla occurs in Professor Lida's study.

15. My colleague Professor J.A. Molinaro called my attention to this Italian folk tale.

16. The Colombian playwright Enrique Buenaventura dramatized "In the Right Hand of the Father" and received highest critical acclaim at the Paris Festival in 1960. (For further details, see Oscar Collazos, "Trayectoria del teatro escuela de Cali," in *Letras Nacionales* [Bogotá], 8 [May - June 1966], 25–27.) Buenaventura's play was translated into English by William I. Oliver under the title "In the Right Hand of God the Father," contained in William I. Oliver's anthology *Voices of Change in the Spanish American Theatre* (Austin, 1971), pp. 171–217.

17. E. M. Forster, *Aspects of the Novel* (London, 1927), p. 142.

18. Rousseau, who regarded Alceste as a tragic figure, was strongly critical of Molière for portraying "so virtuous a character . . . as ridiculous" ("Lettre à M. D'Alembert sur les spectacles" [Paris, 1897], p. 42).

19. Carrasquilla's theme in *Father Casafús* brings two contemporary Colombian novels to mind: *El Cristo de espaldas* (Buenos Aires, 1952) by Eduardo Caballero Calderón and *El día señalado* (Barcelona, 1964) by Manuel Mejía Vallejo. Curcio Altamar has noted a superficial resemblance between Carrasquilla's novel and that of Caballero Calderón. Both protagonists engage in crusades against fanaticism, intolerance, and political intrigue in a rural community. Both are doomed to failure because their extreme individualism and overdeveloped sense of self-importance prevent them from reaching the world around them. Mejía Vallejo's Father Barrios resembles the other two in his fearless stand against corruption and abuse. Yet unlike them, he communicates; his message makes an impact, and his ministry, begun under inauspicious circumstances, has a vitalizing effect.

20. See Frutos in "Simon Magus" (*EPC*, I, 507–517) and Cantalicia in *Long Ago* (*EPC*, II, 211–560).

21. See the introductory paragraph of the novel (*EPC*, I, 175) for a renowned example.

Chapter Five

1. Ricardo Uribe Escobar regards it as "superior to Anatole France's *Petit Pierre*" ("Por Tomás Carrasquilla" in *Política centrífuga* [Medellín, 1960], p. 211).

2. María Teresa Carreño (1853–1917) was a celebrated Venezuelan pianist. Among her compositions was the Venezuelan national anthem.

3. See "A Few Words," preliminary to *Grandeur* (*EPC*, I, 259).

4. Though Doña Juana is the central figure, and Carrasquilla probes most persistently and convincingly into her idiosyncrasies, his own spontaneous affinity with Magola is very evident.

5. *EPC*, II, XVI.

6. The parallel between Carrasquilla's short story and Flaubert's *Un coeur simple* has been noted in *Vida*, pp. 275–76.

7. The motif of a child whose universe becomes tied to trivial objects without material value is a familiar one. Both Benito Lynch's "El potrillo roano" and Benito Pérez Galdós' "La mula y el buey" utilize it in portraying a child who "gives more importance to a toy than to all the things on earth and in heaven." As I pointed out in *Vida*, p. 113, Carrasquilla's version strikes me as more meaningful and universally significant than either of the other two.

8. Lubbock, op. cit., p. 143.

9. See Benito Lynch, *El inglés de los güesos*, 3rd ed. (Madrid, 1930), p. 104.

10. Among Magda Moreno's works are such titles as *El embrujo del micrófono* (Medellín, 1948), *Las hijas de gracia* (Medellín, 1951), and a volume of affectionate reminiscences entitled *Dos novelistas y un pueblo* (Medellín, 1960), devoted to Carrasquilla, Rendón, and the town of Santodomingo.

Chapter Six

1. Nicolás Bayona Posada, *Panorama de la literatura colombiana*, 3rd ed. (Bogotá, 1947), p. 91.

2. Barrios' *El niño que enloqueció de amor* was published in 1915.

3. The pomp and ostentation which characterize the Borja family and which are described with a wealth of narrative detail throw into relief their spiritual illiteracy.

4. Rogelio's overwhelming spiritual experience on a dusty village road in Antioquia bears echoes of Saint Paul's conversion on the road to Damascus, "when suddenly a light from heaven flashed about him" (Acts 9:3).

5. Rafael Maya writes in the prologue to the Argentine edition of the novel: "We believe that Carrasquilla's . . . masterpiece is *The Marchioness of Yolombó*" (*EPC*, II, 16).

6. For a detailed analysis of the novel, see my critical edition of Tomás Carrasquilla, *La Marquesa de Yolombó*, Biblioteca Colombiana, X (Bogotá, 1974), pp. 1–87.

7. The novel is the subject matter of a letter dated February 3, 1932 (*EPC*, II, 803–804) written to Ricardo Uribe Escobar by Carrasquilla's nephew Jorge Arango (on behalf of the ailing author). Arango refers to flattering suggestions on the part of the late Jorge Zalamea, suggestions which the author deprecates with his habitual candor, pointing out that a work as "mediocre as this cannot possibly turn out to be the best of any month." I discussed this point with Zalamea, one of the most exquisite stylists in contemporary Colombian letters, who filled me in on some of the background. It seems that Zalamea, in Spain on a diplomatic assignment at the time, received ten copies of the novel from Colombia for distribution among the "old guard" (Unamuno, Palacio Valdés, etc.). Zalamea, however, with his customary independence, disregarded the instructions and, after cutting out a number of the personal dedications, proceeded to present copies to some of the young writers. Federico García Lorca was a recipient and apparently a very enthusiastic one. (It is easy to see why the renowned Andalusian poet would be impressed with the colourful native element in the book.)

8. Curcio Altamar (p. 166) questions the verisimilitude of the title of marchioness having been conferred upon a woman during the colonial period.

9. The "mass focus" is in my view the major flaw of such a powerful novel as *Huasipungo* by the contemporary Ecuadorean writer Jorge Icaza.

10. Horacio Bejarano Díaz speaks of the affection with which Carrasquilla wrote the novel because it relates to "one of his great-grandfathers" ("Tomás Carrasquilla: novelista del pueblo antioqueño," *Universidad de Antioquia*, XXXI, 122 [June-August 1955], 400–22).

11. See Carlos García Prada's tribute to the character of Bárbara Caballero ("En acción de justicia a Tomás Carrasquilla," in *Estudios hispanoamericanos* [México, 1945], p. 257).

12. Lubbock, op cit., p. 27.

13. In a note appended to Part III of the novel (*EPC*, II, 560), Carrasquilla acknowledges formally the invaluable assistance rendered by certain fellow countrymen.

14. Lubbock, op cit., p. 217.

15. There is a slight discrepancy among the various editions: The 1936 edition gives *Del campo* on the cover and *Del monte* on the title page; the 1952 *Obras completas* edition gives *Del campo* and *EPC* "restores the balance" by giving *Del monte*.

16. *Long Ago*, in this respect, stands alone among Carrasquilla's major works in which tragic denouements predominate.

17. In *EPC*, Parts I and II contain 120 pages each; Part III has 110.

18. The Cuban novelist Alejo Carpentier points out that a novel begins to be great when it ceases to resemble a novel. All the great novels of our time, he adds, have caused the reader to exclaim: "This is not a novel" (*Tientos y diferencias* [La Habana, 1966], p. 13).

Chapter Seven

1. See *Vida*, p. 71.
2. This was the period which witnessed the composition of the essays on the role of movies, bullfighting, and the important three "Simplicities" which are discussed in Chapter 2.
3. I do not have the dates of first publication for either "Titans" or "Salutaris Hostia."
4. The short story "Money Talks" stands first, chronologically, among *Sunday Sketches*.
5. A popular Colombian folk dance.
6. *EPC* prefaces the actual fourteen chronicles entitled "Medellín" with the one called "Hermitage" ("Ermita") which dates from April 15, 1914, and, though dealing with a Medellín site, does not form part of the series, published five years later.
7. The opening sentence of the introductory essay of the set suggests the author's lengthy absence from Medellín (*EPC*, I, 777).
8. See "Memoria científica sobre el cultivo del maíz en los climas cálidos del Estado de Antioquia," *Obras completas de Gregorio Gutiérrez González* (Medellín, 1958), pp. 410–34.

Chapter Eight

1. See *Vida*, ch. VIII.
2. *Historia de la lengua y literatura castellana*, XI (Madrid, 1919), 106.
3. Federico de Onís, Prologue to first edition of *Obras completas* (Madrid, 1952), p. xxv.
4. García Prada's introduction to the volume *Seis cuentos por Tomás Carrasquilla* (México, 1959), pp. 5–30, bears this title.
5. Rafael Maya, Prologue to *The Marchioness of Yolombó* (*EPC*, II, 7).
6. Gerald E. Wade, "An Introduction to the Colombian Novel," *Hispania*, XXX, 4 (November 1947), 472.
7. Curcio Altamar, p. 162.
8. Arturo Torres Ríoseco, *Grandes novelistas de la América Hispana* (Berkeley and Los Angeles, 1949), p. 272.
9. He claimed in his "Autobiography" that *Fruits of my Homeland* was the first realistic novel in Colombia, "taken directly from nature without idealizing in the slightest the reality of life" (*EPC*, I, XXVI).

10. Michael and Mollie Hardwick, *The Charles Dickens Companion* (London, 1965), p. v.

11. T.S. Eliot, *The Use of Poetry and the Use of Criticism* (London, 1933), p. 153.

12. See Maya (*EPC*, II, 15) and Onís (EPC, II, xvi).

13. The fervent plea which Pereda made on behalf of the regional novel during his induction into the Royal Spanish Academy in 1893 (See *Discursos leídos ante la Real Academia Española en la recepción pública del Sr. D. J. M. de Pereda el domingo 21 de febrero de 1893* [Madrid, 1897]) was to be substantially endorsed by Carrasquilla a few years later in "Heresies."

14. Galdós, in replying to his old friend, put his finger on this basic difference between them (*Ibid*).

15. Arturo Uslar Pietri, *Breve historia de la novela hispanoamericana* (Caracas, 1954), p. 170.

16. For details, see my article "Releyendo a María" ("La 'actualidad' de un libro a los cien años de su natalicio"), in *La novela iberoamericana contemporánea* (Caracas, 1968), pp. 341–50.

17. Cejador y Frauca, p. 108.

18. The abortive attempt of his wife to purify his language by "outswearing" him brought Twain's famous retort: "It's no use, my dear. You've got the words but not the music."

19. The Chilean scholar, Arturo Torres Ríoseco, a pioneer in the teaching of Spanish American literature in North America, voiced this prophecy: "The name of the Colombian novelist is growing and soon his fame will be universal in our tongue" ("El nombre del novelista colombiano va creciendo y pronto su fama será universal en nuestro idioma"—"Sobre Tomás Carrasquilla," in *La hebra en la aguja* [México, 1965], p. 115).

Selected Bibliography

(A more extensive bibliography may be found in *Vida*, pp. 289–308.)

PRIMARY SOURCES

1. Editions of Complete Works

Obras completas. Madrid: EPESA, 1952.
Obras completas. Edición Primer Centenario. 2 vols. Medellín: Editorial Bedout, 1958. Rpt. 1964.

2. Editions of Collections (listed in chronological order)

El padre Casafús. Medellín: Carlos E. Rodríquez E., 1914.
Entrañas de niño. Medellín: Carlos E. Rodríguez E., 1914.
Ligia Cruz; Rogelio (Dos novelas cortas). Ediciones Colombia, vol. 13. Bogotá: Ediciones Colombia, 1926.
Dominicales. Medellín: Editorial Atlántida, 1934.
Novelas. Biblioteca Aldeana de Colombia, vol. 12. Bogotá: Editorial Minerva, S.A., 1935.
De tejas arriba. Medellín: Editorial Atlántida, 1936.
Entrañas de niño. Salve, Regina. Biblioteca Popular de Cultura Colombiana, vol. 98. Bogotá: Biblioteca Popular de Cultura Colombiana, 1946.
Cuentos de Tomás Carrasquilla. Ed. by Benigno A. Gutiérrez. Colección Popular de Clásicos Maiceros, vol. IV. Medellín: Editorial Bedout, 1956.
Seis cuentos. Introducción y notas de Carlos García Prada. México: Ediciones de Andrea, 1959. Antologías Studium, vol. 6.
Cuentos. Bolsilibros Bedout, vol. 7. Medellín: Editorial Bedout, 1964.
Cuentos. Medellín: Editorial Montoya, 1968.

3. Editions of Individual Works (listed in chronological order)

Frutos de mi tierra. Bogotá: Librería Nueva, 1896.
Salve, Regina. Medellín: Imprenta Oficial, 1903.
Grandeza. Medellín: La Organización, 1910.
El zarco. Ediciones Colombia, vol. 8. Bogotá: Ediciones Colombia, 1925.
La Marquesa de Yolombó. Medellín: A. J. Cano, 1928.

Grandeza. 2nd ed., Medellín: Imprenta Oficial, 1935.

Hace tiempos (Memorias de Eloy Gamboa). Medellín: Editorial Atlántida, 1935–36.

La Marquesa de Yolombó. Colección Panamericana, vol. 8. Buenos Aires: W. M. Jackson, Inc., 1945.

La Marquesa de Yolombó. Colección Panamericana, vol. 8. 2nd ed., Buenos Aires: W. M. Jackson, Inc., 1946.

Tipos colombianos. Adaptation of Tomás Carrasquilla's Latin American novel *Frutos de mi tierra* by Enrique C. de la Casa and Madge Howe. Educational edition with explanatory Spanish-English vocabulary. 2 vols. Salt Lake City: Department of Modern Languages, University of Utah, 1948.

La Marquesa de Yolombó. Colección Panamericana, vol. 8. 3rd ed., Buenos Aires: W. M. Jackson, Inc., 1957.

La Marquesa de Yolombó. Ministerio de Educación Nacional, División de Extensión Cultural. Bogotá: Litografía Villegas, 1958.

La Marquesa de Yolombó. Biblioteca Básica de Cultura Colombiana, Primera Serie, II. Bogotá: Organización Continental de los Festivales del Libro, 1960.

Salve, Regina. Primer Festival de Autores Antioqueños, 7. Lima: Editora Popular Panamericana, 1961.

La Marquesa de Yolombó. Bolsilibros Bedout, vol. 44. Medellín: Editorial Bedout, 1968.

Frutos de mi tierra. Edición y estudio por Seymour Menton. Biblioteca Colombiana, IV. Bogotá: Instituto Caro y Cuervo, 1972.

La Marquesa de Yolombó. Edición crítica de Kurt L. Levy. Biblioteca Colombiana, X. Bogotá: Instituto Caro y Cuervo, 1974.

SECONDARY SOURCES

1. Critical Material

ARANGO FERRER, JAVIER. *Dos horas de literatura colombiana*. La Tertulia, 6. Medellín: Imprenta Departamental de Antioquia, 1963. A delightfully personal bird's eye view of Colombian letters, both informative and entertaining. The same study formed part of *Panorama das Literaturas das Américas*. 4 vols. Angola: Edicão do Municipio Nova Lisboa, I, II—1958; III—1959; IV—1965, Joaquim Montezuma de Carvalho, ed.

BEJARANO DÍAZ, HORACIO. "Tomás Carrasquilla: novelista del pueblo antioqueño," *Universidad de Antioquia*, XXXI, 122 (June-August 1955), 400–22. A well-documented account of Carrasquilla's major novels—namely, *Frutos de mi tierra*, *Grandeza*, *La Marquesa de Yolombó*, *Hace tiempos*.

CADAVID RESTREPO, TOMÁS. "Tomás Carrasquilla," *Anuario de la Academia Colombiana*. (Bogotá), VIII (1940–1941), 487–503. A warm tribute from one of Carrasquilla's close associates which blends affection with understanding and good taste.

CADAVID URIBE, GONZALO. *Presencia del pueblo en Tomás Carrasquilla*. Biblioteca de Autores Antioqueños, 6. Medellín: Imprenta Departamental de Antioquia, 1959. An informative look at the novelistic world of Tomás Carrasquilla, followed by an index of his character creations with descriptive details. Handy for quick reference.

CURCIO ALTAMAR, ANTONIO. *Evolución de la novela colombiana*. Publicaciones del Instituto Caro y Cuervo, XI. Bogotá: Instituto Caro y Cuervo, 1957. The most authoritative treatment of the subject: a "must" for the researcher of the novel genre in Colombia.

DE ONÍS, FEDERICO. "Tomás Carrasquilla—precursor de la novela americana moderna." Prologue to *Obras completas*, pp. xi–xxv. Madrid: EPESA, 1952. A penetrating analysis of the author, his period, and his region: basic for an understanding of Carrasquilla.

ENGLEKIRK, JOHN E., and GERALD E. WADE. *Bibliografía de la novela colombiana*. México, 1950. (Reprinted and expanded from *Revista Iberoamericana*, No. 30, pp. 301–411.) An essential bibliographical tool which does spade work in a neglected area.

FRANCO, HORACIO. "El diálogo de piedra." in Ernesto González, *Anecdotario de don Tomás Carrasquilla*, pp. 17–24. Medellín: Tipografía Olimpia, 1952. Imaginative glimpses of Carrasquilla's early life by a devoted friend and ardent apologist of Antioquia's cultural values.

GARCÍA PRADA, CARLOS. "Un clásico antioqueño." Prologue to *Seis cuentos*. México: Ediciones de Andrea, 1959. A sensitive evaluation of Carrasquilla's literary art by a pioneer in the teaching of Colombian literature in North America.

GONZÁLEZ, JOSÉ IGNACIO. "La novela y el cuento en Antioquia." In *El pueblo antioqueño*, pp. 329–48. Medellín: Imprenta Universidad, 1942. An informative account of the literary background for Carrasquilla's production.

LEVY, KURT L. "Estudio preliminar." In *La Marquesa de Yolombó*. Edición crítica de Kurt L. Levy. Biblioteca Colombiana, X. Bogotá: Instituto Caro y Cuervo, 1974. An analysis of Carrasquilla's only historical novel.

———*Vida y obras de Tomás Carrasquilla*. Medellín: Editorial Bedout, 1958. The first book length scrutiny of Carrasquilla's life and works.

MAYA, RAFAEL. *Los orígenes del modernismo en Colombia*. Bogotá: Imprenta Nacional, 1961. This splendid book offers, in its final third (Sections IX and X), a thorough analysis of Carrasquilla's position as a literary critic, as reflected in the two *Homilías*.

——— "Tomás Carrasquilla." Prologue to *La Marquesa de Yolombó*. Colección Panamericana, vol. 8. Buenos Aires: W. M. Jackson, Inc.,

1945. A searching study of author and regional background: one of the earliest revaluations of the novelist.

MENTON, SEYMOUR. *"Frutos de mi tierra o Jamones y solomos."* In Tomás Carrasquilla, *Frutos de mi tierra.* Edición y estudio por Seymour Menton. Bogotá: Instituto Caro y Cuervo, 1972. An imaginative analysis which links the two plots of Carrasquilla's first novel in a structural "unity" and reaches the conclusion that *Frutos de mi tierra* is the best novel of the Spanish American realistic school. Menton's study appeared first in *Thesaurus, Boletín del Instituto Caro y Cuervo,* XXV (1970).

————*La novela colombiana: planetas y satélites.* Bogotá: Plaza y Janés, 1978. Thought-provoking interpretations of ten significant Colombian novels (including the article on *Frutos de mi tierra,* published previously in *Thesaurus, Boletín del Instituto Caro y Cuervo,* XXV (1970) and as introductory study to Menton's edition of the novel (Bogotá: Instituto Caro y Cuervo, 1972).

ORJUELA, HÉCTOR. *Fuentes generales para el estudio de la literatura colombiana. Guía bibliográfica.* Bogotá: Instituto Caro y Cuervo, 1968. An invaluable tool for research in Colombian literature; the "most complete source of general reference works . . . in the literature of any Spanish American country."

OSPINA, URIEL. *Sesenta minutos de novela en Colombia.* (Breviarios Colombianos.) Bogotá, no date. A rapid survey including recent literary events, with challenging ideas and some factual inaccuracies. Internal evidence suggests the mid-seventies as approximate date of publication.

RAMOS, OSCAR GERARDO. *De Manuela a Macondo.* (Coleccion de Autores Nacionales.) Bogotá: Instituto Colombiano de Cultura, 1972. Concise accounts of nine well-known Colombian novels, among them an instructive glimpse of *La Marquesa de Yolombó.*

RESTREPO, ANTONIO JOSÉ. *"Del primer novelista antioqueño."* In *Prosas medulares,* 1, 335–48. Barcelona: Editorial Lux, 1919. A fascinating eyewitness account by one of Carrasquilla's classmates at the Universidad de Antioquia in 1876, another distinguished name in Antioqueño prose fiction.

SANÍN CANO, BALDOMERO. *Letras colombianas.* México: Fondo de Cultura Económica, 1944. A succinct but solid view of Colombian literature within its historical and social context.

SYLVESTER, NIGEL. *The "Homilies" and "Dominicales" of Tomás Carrasquilla.* Liverpool: University of Liverpool, Centre for Latin American Studies, 1970. An informative monograph which examines Carrasquilla's critical tenets but fails to take into account Rafael Maya's searching analysis of the *Homilías.*

TORRES RÍOSECO, ARTURO. *"Sobre Tomás Carrasquilla."* In *La hebra en*

la aguja. México: Editorial Cultura, 1965. A brief but perceptive definition of Carrasquilla's artistic worth by one of the veteran teachers
of Latin American literature in the United States.

WADE, GERALD E. "An Introduction to the Colombian Novel," *Hispania*,
XXX, 4 (November 1947), 467–83. A sensitive overview and pioneer
study which recognizes Carrasquilla's eminent position within the context of Colombian letters.

ZALAMEA, JORGE. "Tomás Carrasquilla y David Arthur Thompson." In
"Pórtico," Sunday Literary Supplement to *El Pueblo*, Medellín, January 26, 1941. An ingenious piece of literary trickery from a member
of the Vergara y Vergara Prize jury, which succeeded in confounding
the critics.

2. Background Works

ACOSTA, JOAQUÍN. *Descubrimiento y colonización de la Nueva Granada*.
Bogotá: Imprenta de la Biblioteca Nacional, 1942. A nineteenth century historian's view of the early period in Colombian history. Well
documented.

CIEZA DE LEÓN, PEDRO. *La crónica del Perú*. Biblioteca de Autores Españoles, vol. 26. Madrid: M. Rivadeneyra, 1862. Picturesque glimpses
of the conquest of the Antioqueño region by a sixteenth century Spanish chronicler: a significant source book.

DUQUE BETANCUR, FRANCISCO. *Historia del departamento de Antioquia*.
Medellín: Imprenta Departamental de Antioquia, 1967. The most up
to date general account of Antioquia's history: valuable in spite of the
occasional factual inaccuracy.

FLÓREZ, LUIS. *Habla y cultura popular en Antioquia. Materiales para un
estudio*. Publicaciones del Instituto Caro y Cuervo, vol. 13. Bogotá:
Instituto Caro y Cuervo, 1957. A basic reference work on regional
idiom which draws extensively on Carrasquilla's writings for illustrative
examples.

FRANCO, HORACIO. *Un testimonio y un mensaje*. Medellín: Editorial Gran-
americana, 1963. Verbal portraits of Antioquia's literary figures, drawn
with affectionate pride.

GUTIÉRREZ, BENIGNO A. *Gente maicera (Mosaico de Antioquia la grande)*.
Medellín: Editorial Bedout, 1950. A perceptive introduction to the
geography, culture, and people of Antioquia.

MORENO, MAGDA. *Dos novelistas y un pueblo*. Medellín: Editorial Bedout,
1960. Biographical sketches of Tomás Carrasquilla and Francisco de
Paula Rendón, against the setting of their native village, Santodomingo. Composed by Carrasquilla's niece, the account is colored by local
patriotism.

PARDO TOVAR, ANDRÉS. *El folclore en la obra de Tomás Carrasquilla*.
Ediciones del Centro de Divulgación Pedagógica y Cultural de Boyacá.

Tunja: Imprenta Departamental, 1959. Sensitive treatment of a central component in Carrasquilla's literary art.

PARSONS, JAMES J. *La colonización antioqueña en el occidente de Colombia.* Medellín: Imprenta Departamental de Antioquia, 1950. An authoritative, thoroughly documented enquiry by a North American historian who researched his doctoral dissertation in the region.

El pueblo antioqueño. Medellín: Imp. Universidad, 1942. This informative volume, published to commemorate the fourth centenary of the beginnings of colonization in the region, brings together thirty-two articles on various aspects of Antioqueño history and culture.

RESTREPO, PADRE HUBERTO. *La religión de la antigua Antioquia.* Medellín: Editorial Bedout, 1972. A thought-provoking, anthropological approach to the place of religion in Antioqueño life, as reflected in eight of Carrasquilla's novels.

ROMOLI, KATHLEEN. *Colombia, Gateway to South America.* Garden City, N.Y.: Doubleday, Doran & Co., Inc., 1941. A splendidly readable introduction to Colombian geography and life: a very useful book in spite of its age.

URIBE ANGEL, MANUEL. *Geografía general y compendio histórico del estado de Antioquia en Colombia.* Paris: Imprenta de Victor Goupy y Jourdan, 1885. A pioneer work: old but indispensable for an understanding of the spirit of the region.

URIBE URIBE, RAFAEL. *Diccionario abreviado de galicismos, provincialismos y correcciones de lenguaje.* Medellín: Imprenta del Departamento, 1887. A major exploration of the regional idiom by a renowned military and political figure.

Index